D-DAY DIARY

D-DAY DIARY

LIFE ON THE FRONT LINE IN THE SECOND WORLD WAR

CAROL HARRIS

The History Press

First published 2013

An exclusive edition for The Works
Midpoint Park, Minworth, Sutton Coldfield, B76 1RN

The History Press
The Mill, Brimscombe Port
Stroud, Gloucestershire, GL5 2QG
www.thehistorypress.co.uk

British Library Cataloguing in Publication Data.
A catalogue record for this book is available from the British Library.

ISBN 978 0 7509 6196 7

Typesetting and origination by The History Press
Printed in Great Britain

Contents

Acknowledgements

The Allied landings in Normandy on D-Day, 6 June 1944 marked the beginning of the end of the Second World War. This short book tells the story of the event through the accounts of eyewitnesses.

Today, the D-Day invasion is viewed as not only the biggest but also the most successful invasion ever launched. These contemporary accounts show that at the time, such an outcome seemed far from certain.

As far as I have been able to ascertain, all of those whose accounts make up this book survived the war, although few, sadly, are alive today.

I would like to thank the following people who gave me permission to quote from their own or their relatives' accounts: Sheila Austin, Barbara Beal, the family of Maureen Bolster, W. Cutler, Annette Conway (for extracts from the papers of Rev. Leslie Skinner), A.M. Kerr (for the account by Captain Maurice Jupp), and Patricia Wildman. Also, to Olivia Beattie at Biteback Publishing, and to the following for permission to quote from online sources: Patrick Elie of the 6Juin website, Mark Hickman of the Pegasus Archive, Lew Johnston from the Air Mobility Command Museum, H. Kalliomaki at Veterans Affairs Canada, the Black Hills Veterans Writing Group, Andrew Whitmarsh of the D-Day Museum in Portsmouth, and Paul Zigo and Donna Bastedo of Center for World War II Studies and Conflict Resolution.

Acknowledgements

I am especially grateful to the following, without whom this book could not have been written: William and Ralph for their administrative support; Mike Brown for his expert advice; Sophie Bradshaw and Lindsey Smith of The History Press for keeping the project on track, and staff at the Imperial War Museum Research Room, especially Simon Offord, Documents and Sound Archivist.

Abbreviations

AA	Anti-aircraft
ack-ack	Anti-aircraft guns ( )
ADS	Advanced Dressing Station
APM	Assistant Provost Marshal
ARK	Armoured Ramp Carrier
ARV	Armoured Reconnaissance Vehicle
ASR	Air Sea Rescue
AVRE	Armoured Vehicle, Royal Engineers
BM	Beachmaster
Brig. Gen.	Brigadier General
Capt.	Captain
CIGS	Chief of the Imperial General Staff
CO	Commanding Officer
Col	Colonel
DD tanks	Duplex Drive tanks
DUKW	Six-wheeled amphibious vehicle
DZ	Drop Zone
EME	Electrical and Mechanical Engineers
ENSA	Entertainments National Service Association
FANY	First Aid Nursing Yeomanry
Fd Sqn	Field Squadron
FM	Field Marshal
FUSAG	First United States Army Group
FW	Focke-Wulf

Gen.	General
Grp Capt.	Group Captain
GT	General Transport
HAA	Heavy Anti-Aircraft
HE	High Explosive
IC	In charge (of)
IO	Intelligence Officer
LAA	Light Anti-Aircraft
LCA	Landing Craft, Assault
LCI (L)	Landing Craft, Infantry (Large)
LCM	Landing Craft, Mechanised
LCP	Landing Craft, Personnel
L/Cpl	Lance Corporal
LCR	Landing Craft Rocket
LCT	Landing Craft, Tank
LCT(R)	Landing Craft, Tank (Rocket)
LCVP	Landing Craft Vehicle, Personnel
L/Sgt	Lance Sergeant
L/Sgt	Lance Sergeant
LST	Landing Ship Tank
Lt Col	Lieutenant Colonel
Lt	Lieutenant
Maj. Gen.	Major General
Maj.	Major
m/c	Motorcycle
Me	Messerscmitt
MG	Machine Gun
MI5	British intelligence agency
ML	Motor Launch
MO	Medical Officer
NAAFI	Navy, Army and Air Force Institutes
NCO	Non-Commissioned Officer

OC	Officer Commanding
PIAT	Projector, Infantry, Anti-Tank
PO	Pilot Officer
RAF	Royal Air Force
RA	Royal Artillery
RASC	Royal Army Service Corps
REME	Royal Electrical and Mechanical Engineers
RE	Royal Engineers
Rev	Reverend
RM	Royal Marines
RN	Royal Navy
RNVR	Royal Naval Volunteer Reserve
R/T	Radio Telegraph
RV	Rendezvous
SBG	Small Box Girder
Sgt	Sergeant
SHAEF	Supreme Headquarters Allied Expeditionary Force
Spr	Sapper
SP	Self-propelled
Sqn Ldr	Squadron Leader
TCG	Troop Carrier Group
TCS	Troop Carrier Squadron
Tp	Troop
TSM	Temporary Sergeant Major
Wg Cdr	Wing Commander
W/Ops	Wireless Operators
WRNS	Women's Royal Naval Service
W/T	Secret messages transmitted by Morse Code

Glossary

Abwehr German military intelligence
Aldis lamp lamp used for signalling
Bangalore/Bangalore torpedo a series of tubes filled with explosive, used to clear barbed wire and minefields
Blockships craft which were deliberately sunk to create a 'gooseberry'
Bobbin device fitted to an AVRE for unrolling a reinforced canvas carpet over barbed wire or soft ground
Bofors anti-aircraft and multi-purpose gun
Bostick waterproofing
Bren light machine gun
Compo field rations
Crab Sherman tank fitted with a rotating cylinder and chains for exploding mines
Crocodile Churchill tank with a flamethrower in place of the more usual machine gun
E-boats German high-speed torpedo boats
Element 'C' barrier Cointet-element, also known as a Belgian Gate. A mobile anti-tank obstacle, comprising a heavy steel fence usually mounted on concrete rollers. Part of the German defences on the beaches
Fascine bundle of brushwood poles, launched from an AVRE and used to fill gaps
Flail device attached to a vehicle for clearing mined areas

Gooseberry an area of sheltered water created from groups of ships scuttled off each of the landing beaches
H-Hour time at which operation begins
Hawkin's grenade anti-tank hand grenade
Hedgehog Landing Craft Assault Hedgehog: an adapted Royal Navy landing craft which fired a barrage of spigot mortars on to the beach, to clear mines and other obstructions. It can also refer to an anti-tank beach obstacle
Landing craft vessels which conveyed the landing force infantry and vehicles from ships to the shore. Most had serial numbers, not names
Liberty ships argo ships built and supplied by the USA
Luftwaffe German airforce
M10 tank destroyer
ML motor launch
Mulberry prefabricated, temporary harbour made in sections and towed across the English Channel Phoenix – reinforced hollow concrete chambers which formed breakwaters
Oerlikon anti-aircraft cannon
Rhino modified tank
Slidex manual card-based coding system
Sten submachine gun
Tetrahedron beach obstacle
Teller Mine/Tellermine anti-tank mine
TNT explosive
Wehrmacht combined armed forces of Germany

1

Testing and Training

The early years of the Second World War were marked by the rapid advance of Germany and Japan as they swept through Europe and the Pacific regions. By the end of 1940, most of Western Europe was under Nazi rule and Britain stood alone. Japan, Germany and Italy had signed the Tripartite Pact, establishing them as the Axis Powers and guaranteeing mutual support if any one of them were to be attacked by any country other than the Soviet Union.

It became increasingly obvious, as the years passed, that an invasion of mainland Europe by the Allies would be necessary to secure victory and end the war. American involvement was essential: without their resources – equipment and soldiers – Britain could only hope to stay in less-than-splendid isolation, cut off from Europe. There, its closest neighbours – France, the Netherlands and Belgium – were under Nazi control, and others such as Switzerland, Portugal and Spain remained neutral.

The Japanese attack on the US base in Pearl Harbor in December 1941 changed the picture dramatically, forcing the United States, in which anti-war sentiment had been a strong influence, to enter the war. This meant that, suddenly, the Allies had enough manpower and equipment to make an invasion possible, although nothing on the scale required had ever been attempted before.

Allied plans for an invasion of Northern France were first outlined in Operation Roundup in 1942. The plan was drawn up by President Eisenhower, then Brigadier General of the US forces, and the invasion was to take place in early 1943. It quickly became apparent, however, that this was unlikely to happen: among British objections were those of Winston Churchill, who favoured an invasion through the Mediterranean, and those of British military chiefs, who wanted to wait until the German Army was worn down by fighting in the Soviet Union.

Samuel Eliot Morison, an American historian and sailor in the US Navy, wrote in his book *The Invasion of France and Germany* that, given shortages of merchant shipping, landing craft and other resources, the planned date of early 1943 was unrealistic. Any such invasion called for a force of between 500,000 and 750,000 soldiers and 5,800 aircraft. British and Allied forces from the rest of Europe would have to await the arrival of US forces and equipment, which would have to be sent by sea and air across the Atlantic.

Operation Bolero, the codename for this build-up of military personnel and equipment, began at the end of April 1942. Over the next two years, soldiers, sailors and airmen drawn from Britain, America, Canada, Australia, New Zealand, the Netherlands, France, Belgium, Norway, Poland and Czechoslovakia were trained and organised into the largest invasion force ever seen.

Naturally, the build-up of such enormous forces required an extraordinary level of secrecy.

If the German Army discovered the true date and location of the invasion of Europe, it could plan a response and inflict heavy casualties on the invading forces.

Landing craft waiting to leave England. (Author)

There was ample evidence of the catastrophe which could follow a botched invasion. In August 1942, an Allied raid was attempted on the French port of Dieppe. The invading force totalled more than 6,000 troops, included 5,000 Canadians, 1,000 British Commandos and fifty American Rangers. They were supported by eight Allied destroyers and seventy-four Allied air squadrons. The aims were to gather information and destroy equipment and installations.

The Allies knew little about their target. The town and beaches were heavily defended by 1,500 German infantry with machine guns and artillery. Over 60 per cent of those – mainly Canadian – forces who went ashore were killed, wounded or taken prisoner. The only success of the nine-hour raid was the capture, by commandos under Lord Lovat, of a gun battery. Losses among the RAF and Navy were high too.

Kenneth Beal, a signalman with the Light Coastal Forces of the Royal Navy, was on the raid in Motor Launch 194. He wrote later:

> The old timers on board, who knew the drill for these occasions, found time to give themselves a thorough wash all over. Then they changed their underwear and replaced it with the clean items. Why? Because, they said, many wounds were made worse by fragments of dirty clothing carried into them. I sobered up a bit at this point. Most of us copied them.
>
> Before dawn, we saw tracer fire up ahead between our leading ships and a German coastal convoy. It lasted about 15 minutes and I wondered what the enemy's look-outs ashore would make of it. A little later came the sound of our aircraft passing overhead as the early grey light began to lift the darkness.
>
> We had, by this time, passed safely through the Germans' minefields. Our sweepers up ahead had cleared a path for us, dropping small lighted buoys to mark the swept channel. Red to port and green to starboard.
>
> The sound of bombing ahead commenced, and gradually crescendoed. The sky lightened and we could

see smoke from the land, and debris being hurled high into the air. The exchange of fire between the Van [vanguard] of our forces and the shore began slowly. It grew in intensity until, in what was now bright light, we ourselves, accompanied by the orchestra of battle came into the fight …

My fear was made worse by the unbearably slow approach to the beach and the guns. This creeping approach was very hard on my nerves. I found that something was pulling me strongly in the other direction, and if I had been a soldier on land, I would have run for it. At this point we did turn for the open sea, but only to go back and get one of the LCP's and give her a tow.

The crew of ML 214 who were leading the group told me after, that when they saw us turn tail and speed out to sea again, they felt very bad. Actually it made me feel better. It was only a temporary retreat and we had to cross that nasty stretch of water a second time before we rejoined the group.

The shells were now exploding right in amongst our LCPs. 'Poor Devils' I thought when one was almost capsized by one of the huge shells. It righted itself however and carried on in. Then clearly across the water from the Canadians came the boost to my morale that I so badly needed.

BAGPIPES. In peacetime I disliked them. On that morning they were music indeed. The Camerons of Canada's piper was playing his wild music to take his regiment in to the beach to face the enemy.

ML 214 had originally headed in slightly to the west of where she should have been. Discovering her error in time she altered course slightly to the east, approaching the correct beach diagonally. Not very good navigating at about 6.00am on a bright and sunny morning.

At about this time the big guns that had been harassing us ceased their firing.

We thought that we had by then got in so close that the guns, high on the cliffs, could not depress down on to us. I read later that our commandos had gone in ahead of the Camerons, scaled the cliffs up to the gun emplacements, and after a short but desperate fight had silenced the guns and their crews. This was one of the few successes of the day. Good old Lord Lovat and his bonny men.

Over on the other side of the assault area the Free French Chasseurs, smallish craft though bigger than MLs, were carrying the Marines. This I heard from Sparks during the morning, together with the fact that the Marines did not get ashore. If that is so, I do not know the reason why.

We had no idea how the battle in general was going. Jerry had apparently only recently reinforced his defences with extra troops, and was ready and waiting for the Canadians to come to him. The Canadians stood little chance.

During the morning the Germans, clever as ever, started using the Canadian radio frequencies and call signs that our lot were using, which they must have gained knowledge of through their monitoring.

They issued confusing orders and contradictory instructions, probably using renegade Frenchmen, and this did not help our lot one bit.

Sapper Vic Sparrow of the Royal Canadian Engineers was one of the Canadian troops who took part in the assault:

I hit the beach and everything was just going like crazy. I just curled up and I don't think I moved a muscle for a while. I would peek out and all of a sudden I would see a guy a little piece away from me and he'd look up and the next thing he was gone. He got it. It was that way. Finally things did quieten down a bit. I got up and walked along the beach a piece and I covered up this one chap and covered up a couple of lads. A fella by the name of Billy Lynch, who was in my outfit, he started to write a book. I got a copy of the transcript and in it he said he looked up, he was down by this timber, and he looked up and saw Lieutenant Shackelton and Sapper Sparrow running up and down the beach. He said the crazy so and so's, they're going to get killed. Well I didn't get killed. I didn't get a scratch as far as that was concerned. But, I saw one chap when he tried to go over the wire, he got hit and he was just burned to a crisp right there. It was almost impossible to move without getting hit.

Private John Patrick Grogan, from the Central Ontario Regiment, was also pinned down by heavy German fire.

We knew what we were supposed to do all right. We were to get to land and get over the beach as quickly as we could and get up over the sea wall. But on landing, I guess the first thing I recall is that some of the people who had landed before me . . . there was the beach lined with people all lying there. And the stones. There were big stones, huge stones on that beach. And it seemed to me to be crazy for these people to be lying down there. We had a habit in manoeuvres, you'd run so far then you'd duck down or you might crawl a bit. But I just couldn't understand what they were all lying there for. But they were dead. They were either dead or they had all been hit. I got up near the sea wall and near the sea wall you were fairly safe. But out from the sea wall six or seven feet there was no one living. So these people that were down by the water's edge when I went off had all been hit. And the ones that I had waved good-bye to that morning, and the ones we had joked with such as Sammy Adams, he was one of the first that I saw, Joe Coffey, Huey Clements, Ernie Good, all of these people all dead in such a short space of time …

Then I heard a loud speaker. The fellow talking English with an accent, a German accent. But he spoke perfect English. He said that we didn't have a chance, 'to throw down your arms'. He called us brave Canadians and he said, 'throw down your arms and surrender', and that the wounded would be taken care of, or else we would be annihilated. Then I heard someone say, going running by, the word 'surrender', you see. I ventured out from where I was and could see down a piece a group of people with white bandages and an odd white towel and with their hands up. Things began to get quiet. Just as if there was a great stillness. After all of this noise, everything stopped for a bit.

Someone else, took a look out and they said that the beach was swarming with German soldiers.

On his motor launch, Kenneth Beal watched events unfold:

We went alongside a Tank Landing Craft, which was slowly sinking … The Canadian major on board had seen three Canadian tanks go up the beach and get knocked out in seconds. The enemy fire had been sweeping the beach so intensely that he would not send his infantry to follow them to certain death. Good guy that officer.

Before that TLC backed off she was hit a number of times. Her bridge took four direct hits. All the upper deck Navy crew were either killed or critically wound. Except for the skipper. He, poor man, was only just in control, shaking like a leaf. But he hadn't got a scratch on him. We took off all the injured. All were stretchered. Their sick bay Tiffy [sick berth attendant] told our lads that some were dying.

The Canadians were now manning the TLC's guns.

We pulled away from her to take the wounded to a destroyer, which had sick bay facilities. After we had passed over those casualties, we pushed off again on our rather aimless patrol. I was glad because I instinctively thought it a bad idea to form even small clusters of ships. They made a better target for the Luftwaffe.

On shore there was any amount of noise going on. We moved slowly about on a flat calm sea. I saw our Boston Bombers coming in from England. Skimming in low over the waves to hit their targets ashore …

Soon after midday we took in tow a small landing craft, drifting without power, with one petty officer on board, and towed him all the way back to Newhaven. Some time after 2.30pm, our people decided that enough was enough and preparations were made to leave. Many Canadians were left on shore to be captured. The force brought back some prisoners.

The raid was a failure, but it taught us the folly of trying to land directly at a port, and on its nearby beaches.

Our boat was the last of the flotilla to enter Newhaven, at 11:30pm. Our Base staff, worried stiff, were there to greet us. They told us that they had spent part of the day on the breakwater listening to the distant thunder coming from Dieppe, sixty miles away. Our late arrival back brought them on board to welcome us. It was touching to suddenly realise that we meant something to them.

A few days later, on the train going into Brighton, I noticed some Canadians in the same carriage as me. They were looking tired and dishevelled, and fed up.

One of them was wearing a Canadian shoulder flash and I tried to open conversation with him. Well, as we had been on the other side together, up to a point, I thought that I could say Hallo at least. He however was very tight lipped, so I dropped the attempt. That incident has always worried me a little. Was his reluctance to talk because he had lost a friend and hadn't recovered from the shock? Had they been told 'No talking'? Or, and this is a slightly guilty feeling on my part, had ML 214, going into the beach in the first instance in the wrong place, given the Canadians trouble we hadn't heard about? I only hope that it was not the latter.

The next day, on the train to Newhaven I shared a carriage with some civilian workmen on their way to work. They were talking loudly and knowing about the raid, and a lot of drivel it was. One chap said that he had seen our cruisers exploding, and I tore into them verbally. I was still feeling raw under the surface about the mess it had been, I only know that the wild inaccuracies they were putting forward as facts, made me very angry, and I overreacted.

Dieppe was studied carefully in the planning of the invasion, and by 1944, techniques, equipment and tactics had changed. Some Allied military leaders, including Vice-Admiral Louis Mountbatten, the British Chief of Combined Operations, who planned the raid, said that it had given valuable lessons. Others, such as General Sir Leslie Hollis, who was Secretary to the Chiefs of Staff Committee and deputy head of the military wing of the War Cabinet, thought it an unmitigated disaster and that its lessons would have been learned in other, less costly ways.

Dieppe was seen as a model of what not to do in an invasion. A crucial factor had been the lack of surprise. German prisoners captured at Dieppe told their interrogators that they had known in advance the date and time of the raid through information from French double agents.

The New York Times of 8 June 1942 carried the headline, 'Warning By Radio; Notice of "Likely" War Moves Given Civilians in Nazi-Held Zone', and reported that 'French civilians were urged by Britain today to evacuate quickly the Atlantic coastal districts of occupied France'.

The raid showed the Allies that capturing a well-defended, major port in through which the invasion forces could advance was impractical and so artificial Mulberry harbours were developed.

Dieppe also showed the need for specially adapted tanks to cope with beach defences. At the time of the raid, work was well underway designing and testing such weapons. The tanks were operated by the 79th Armoured Division and specialists from the Royal Engineers, under the command of Major General Sir Percy Hobart.

Hobart had been one of the first to understand the potential of tanks and the new tactics which would make their deployment decisive in battle. Rather than follow the traditional defensive approach of trench warfare, he and other 'radicals', such as the military strategist Basil Liddell Hart, argued for a new mobile approach in which tanks would play a crucial role. Hobart's view, characteristically blunt, was: 'Why piddle about making porridge with artillery and then send men to drown themselves in it for a hundred yards of No Man's Land? Tanks mean advances of miles at a time, not yards.'

Between the two world wars, Hobart had continued to develop his theories and, in 1934, he was put in charge of the first permanent armoured brigade in the British Army. In 1938 he was sent to train the new 'mobile force Egypt', which later became the 7th Armoured Division, better known as the 'Desert Rats'.

He was internationally renowned, especially by the German military, whose senior officers used his tactics with great success during the invasion of France and the Low Countries from May 1940 onwards. But Hobart's radicalism and irascible manner made him widely unpopular with the traditionalist majority in the British Army. As a result, Percy Hobart was retired by General Archibald Wavell in 1940 and became a lance corporal in the Home Guard. In August 1940, as Britain worried about a German invasion, Basil Liddell Hart wrote in the *News Chronicle* of 'Britain's wasted brains', singling out Hobart as the prime example. After Prime Minister Winston Churchill read the article, he insisted that Hobart be given an armoured division to command. There was fierce resistance from Hobart's military contemporaries and, in October 1940, Churchill wrote to Sir John Dill, the Chief of the Imperial General Staff:

> I was very pleased last week when you told me you proposed to give an armoured division to General Hobart. I think very highly of this officer, and I am not at all impressed by the prejudices against him in certain quarters. Such prejudices attach frequently to persons of strong personality and original view. In this case, General Hobart's views have been only too tragically borne out. The neglect by the General Staff even to devise proper patterns of tanks before the war has robbed us of all the fruits of this invention. These fruits have been reaped by the enemy, with terrible consequences. We should, therefore, remember that this was an officer who had the root of the matter in him, and also vision. I have carefully read your note to me, and the summary of the case for and against General Hobart. We are now at war, fighting for our lives, and we cannot afford to confine Army appointments to officers who have excited no hostile comment in their career. The catalogue of General Hobart's qualities and defects might almost exactly be attributed to any of the great commanders of British history.
>
> ... This is a time to try men of force and vision, and not be confined exclusively to those who are judged thoroughly safe by conventional standards.

Hobart set to work and, in March 1943, Field Marshal Alanbrooke, Dill's successor as CIGS, put Hobart in charge of developing the specialist vehicles which would move the battle off the beaches and inland as quickly as possible.

At the beginning of 1944, Alanbrooke went to see the progress made:

> 27 January, 1944
> Eisenhower met me at the station last night and we travelled up by special train through the night. Hobart collected us at 9 am and took us first to his HQ where he showed us his models, and his proposed assault organisation. We then went on to see various exhibits such as the Sherman tank for destroying tank mines, with chains on a drum driven by the engine, various methods of climbing walls with tanks, blowing up of minefields and walls, flame throwing Churchill tanks, wall destroying engineer parties, floating tanks, teaching men how to escape from sunken tanks, etc, etc. A most interesting day, and one which Eisenhower seemed to enjoy thoroughly. Hobart has been doing wonders in his present job and I am delighted that we put him into it.

Trooper Austin Baker was a wireless operator in C Squadron, 4th/7th Royal Dragoon Guards, 8th Armoured Brigade, and in 1945, wrote of his time in 'Hobart's Funnies':

> In April 1944 I was put on the Squadron's Armoured Recovery Vehicle, a turretless Sherman fitted with gas welding equipment, towing bars and all kinds of fitters' paraphernalia. It was intended to carry a kind of flying squad of fitters and I was to be its wireless operator …

Allied forces were based all over the UK rehearsing the invasion as plans and preparations gathered pace. Troops were trained to use specialised equipment and tactics were tested and revised. Assault infantry, armoured and airborne troops could train in small and large numbers. Naval, air and army support units needed large-scale exercises to test their abilities. Early results showed communication problems and a general sense of chaos.

In 1943, Major John Rex, serving with the Royal Engineers Movement Control Section, had begun work on movement control plans for D-Day, initially with the 3rd Division in Scotland and 51st (Highland) Division in England. Training often took place in the worst weather conditions, such as this exercise on the low-lying Black Isle of Cromarty, which Major Rex wrote about in his memoirs after the war:

> In these winter days it had a barren and wild look and the men suffered extreme hardships from snow, sleet and intense cold winds. They had heather for a bed, food was iron rations and cigarettes were short; it was comfortless training, but they soldiered through it magnificently.
>
> Embarked, they passed another night between the steel walls of landing craft, exposed to rough seas and victims of seasickness, but training had made these men hard as iron and as tough as steel, and the following morning when the beach landing was on, they had recovered. They jumped into the sea; they waded ashore, through icy cold waters. It was bleak enough observing the operation from cover on the beach top.
>
> … Full-blooded conferences were taking place now in the hall at the barracks, with the Admiral and the General and other high staff officers on the platform.
>
> We got advice on almost everything from a cure for seasickness to how to die respectfully and what to do to an enemy before one died …
>
> We criticised some utterances of our seniors, tore them from their words, then patched them up again. We praised

and we damned. We all knew that the assaulting infantry would be taking a bloody hard knock when invasion day came.

But our talks always ended on the same note, that it was going to be a fine party.

George, my near bedmate, hinted that very likely he would die of fright.

In our offices this continuous planning sometimes got us under the weather; there were so many difficulties and so many opinions expressed on how to overcome them ...

We had to stand up and ventilate our thoughts against brotherly opposition; words meant everything – no mere talk in these Highlands.

The War Office were pouring print upon us, giving the results of secret trials, verbatim reports of the latest intelligence obtained from enemy sources and vital changes in the planning.

These were minor conferences every day, visits of junior commanders, queries on weights and measurements of vehicles and capacities of landing craft.

The thinking and work went on all day and into the night, every day, seven days a week.

...Winter was coming to an end, when the day arrived for the final exercise, that of a complete divisional beach landing.

... I was going ashore with rear headquarters an hour after lunch ... We all slipped overboard. What a joke, promised a dry landing!

I went down to my shoulders; lucky me, six feet tall – an awful cold sensation gripped my tummy, the shock must have given my face the blues.

Others went clean under – small fellows. One, a signals clerk disappeared holding his Sten and map case above his head. We took hold of ourselves, we quickly gripped hands together and plunged ashore somehow, like half drowned rats.

The receding tide was trying strongly to pull us back. It was an awkward five minutes …

We were soaking, with a winter evening soon to fall.

The sea oozed out of us, as we walked along; we were a good joke for those already on the beach.

We agreed the air was bracing. Where was headquarters?

Someone had the map location and we decided on our direction, finding we had between four and five miles to tramp.

We couldn't possibly make it before dark.

It was cold now, a timid sun was fast declining; we shivered in our wet state, then pulled ourselves together and cut inland over a territory of baby fir trees.

Clearing this we were amongst the infantry, the guns and the armour.

Unit transport was everywhere and men were digging in for the night.

We walked on, out of this influence into the open country and now and again were engaged in boy time sport of jumping ditches.

Night fell; there was another mile to go and entering headquarters at last we sat in right away on the General's conference on the beaching operation.

The room was full of officers dripping wet, but not much concerned with this state, many only anxious to have a cigarette. My packets were running water.

Slapton Sands

Parts of the British coast that mimicked the conditions the invading forces were likely to encounter in France were commandeered for training. In Devon, Slapton Sands was a major practice area and, in November 1943, all those living in the surrounding villages – 3,000 people – were told they would have to leave their homes by 20 December. American ships arrived as the residents left and training began in earnest.

Exercise Tiger, conducted between 22 and 30 April 1944, was one such rehearsal. Landing ships and craft left Plymouth, Dartmouth and Brixham fully loaded with men, vehicles and live ammunition. This simulation of the crossing to France was followed by a bombardment and an invasion of the beach at Slapton Sands. The landings began on the morning of 27 April.

Barbara Bruford was in the Women's Royal Naval Service (WRNS, also known as 'Wrens'). In 1944 she was serving at nearby Portland Bill on the south coast, listening to German transmissions across the Channel:

> Looking back now, it seems amazing that we were not more surprised by some of the happenings around us. One of the most alarming to me occurred some weeks before [D-Day]. A local army intelligence officer came calling at my office to ask whether I, or any one of the other Wrens, could read Morse by flash. Rashly, I said that I could.
>
> The good old service maxim 'never volunteer' came back to me too late. On the cliffs below the quarries was an old disused lighthouse, largely in ruins, but with one

or two rooms still habitable. A young couple had taken up residence there, which was odd, as this was a military restricted zone. Some of the local fishermen hauling crab pots off the Bill had reported seeing lights flashing at night from the building. Portlanders are strange, suspicious people and they were sure that there was an enemy surface craft getting messages sent to it about the shipping in the harbour.

Would I be prepared to help them to make sure what was going on? Being young and keen and somewhat thick, I agreed. That night I dressed up in dark slacks, jersey and balaclava helmet and went out on to the cliffs with the soldiery where we crawled into a good place to see what was going on. The army retreated, leaving me lying alone on a windy cliff in the dark, with my field glasses at the ready. I was never the stuff of which intrepid female spies are made and frankly I was scared rigid, expecting every minute to be bashed over the head by some brutal Nazi. Fortunately it was not a very long wait, the occupants of the lighthouse did indeed start flashing a message and I saw an answering flash from out at sea. After all this time I do not remember whether it was code or plain language, but I do recall that it was German naval procedure that was used. I retreated hastily and called up the troops who made a quick raid and caught the couple red-handed. Not many days after this, we all saw the disastrous 'Operation Tiger' … On the night it happened, a watchkeeper coming on duty said, 'Ma'am you should go outside – something is going on.' I went out on the cliff to see three large ships ablaze in the West Bay off Start Point, with shells and machine gun fire going off all round them. We of course thought that it was one of the convoys being attacked. We heard no E-boat traffic that night in spite of very diligent searching by the watch.

Several days later, I had occasion to go into the dockyard, where I saw bodies stacked up under tarpaulins like firewood. Then I heard from staff officers the real story. It had been an exercise in West Bay which had gone wrong. Practically a whole US division had been lost.

The Americans have always maintained that E-boats attacked and torpedoed their troopships and that we didn't pass on the information to them that the E-boats were operating, but what is certain is that the Americans lost their heads in the crisis and fired on each other. Many of the GIs were very young and had no survival training. The Portland MO told me that many of them had died unnecessarily because of exposure in the lifeboats, or drowned because they had put their lifejackets on incorrectly.

A group of German E-boats (high-speed torpedo boats) spotted a convoy on the exercise and attacked three landing ship tanks. Hundreds of men, mainly US soldiers, died in the ships, trapped below decks. More died after in the sea of hypothermia, or by drowning. In total, 749 American soldiers and sailors lost their lives. Changes were made: radio frequencies were standardised; troops were given better life jacket training and plans were laid for small craft to pick up survivors during the invasion.

2

Deception and Delay

Deception as to the real location of the landings was crucial to the success of the invasion. If the Germans knew where the invasion was to take place, they would be able to concentrate troops and equipment in the area and the invasion could fail, like the raid on Dieppe, on the beaches. Conversely, creating as much confusion as possible about the likely target area for the invasion landings would force the Germans to spread troops and equipment throughout their extensive territory.

Double agents – spies apparently working for the Germans but actually reporting to British intelligence – played an essential part in the multitude of deception operations undertaken before D-Day. One of the most famous was Juan Pujol García, codenamed 'Garbo' by the British. With his MI5 case officer Tomás Harris, Garbo set up a fictional network of fellow spies who fed him information, which he then passed on to his German handlers.

On 4 May 1944, Harris discussed his plan for Garbo in Operation Fortitude, the codename for the Allies' deception tactics, aimed at misleading the Germans as to where the invasion would land:

> There will, we hope, be among the leaders of Germany some who will draw the conclusion we are trying to

inspire through Fortitude. If we can continue through Garbo and the Abwehr to supply those Germans who are already inclined to believe in our cover plan with further ammunition for our arguments … it may well be that we shall be helping those elements in Germany to influence plans in our favour during the few critical days of the post-assault period.

Over the next few weeks, Garbo sent a stream of false information 'gathered' from his non-existent spy network, to the Abwehr about the build-up of troops and the location of the invasion. Even after the invasion had landed, his and other spies' efforts dissuaded the Germans from counter-attacking immediately because they continued to believe that the landings were a diversion from the main landings, which would be in the Pas-de-Calais.

Operation Copperhead, played out seven weeks before the landings, was another successful deception. Its principal participant was Maynard Clifton James, an Australian soldier in the Army Pay Corps; he was a professional actor in civilian life and resembled Field Marshal Montgomery. James was called for an interview, ostensibly for a part in an Army training film. However, after asking him to sign the Official Secrets Act, the officer interviewing James said:

'I have nothing to do with Army films. I am a member of MI5, the Army Intelligence branch … You have been chosen to act as the double of General Montgomery,' he said quietly. 'I am in charge of this job. It is our business to trick the enemy and perhaps save the lives of thousands of men … I have no idea of the date of the invasion, but there is no time to be lost. We shall train you to play

> your part, and when the time comes for you to go on the stage, you will be General Montgomery … You will impersonate Monty in Great Britain while he himself goes abroad to launch an invasion in the Mediterranean.'
>
> As I discovered later, this was not true. It was a reversal of the actual plans which were only disclosed to me at the last possible moment. At that time they did not know if I was capable of keeping my mouth shut and so there was a double reason why they should play for safety. If, in fact, I allowed the secret to leak out, the Germans would learn the very story which MI5 were hoping to plant in their minds.

The American general George Patton was as famous as Montgomery at this time. Like Montgomery, Patton was frequently photographed, quoted in the press and heard on the radio. As a result, he had a dual role in the invasion plans.

In his diary for 26 January 1944, Patton wrote:

> Called on Ike [Eisenhower] at office and found I am to command Third Army. All are novices and in support of Bradley's First Army – not such a good job, but better than nothing … Well, I have an Army and it is up to me. 'God show the right'. As far as I can remember, this is my twenty-seventh start from zero since entering the U.S. Army. Each time I have made a success of it, and this one must be the biggest.

It was difficult for Patton to keep the necessary low profile in his work getting the US Third Army ready to fight in France.

On 20 February, he wrote to his wife Beatrice:

> Yesterday I went into Butch's room and ran into the whole press, so I just told them I was a ghost and they admitted everyone in town had seen me, no one would admit it. I wish I could stop being incognito but really it makes no difference as I am a very apparent entity.

A few weeks later, on 6 March, he wrote to her again:

> This damned secrecy thing is rather annoying particularly as I doubt if it fools any one. Every time I make a speech I have to say now remember you have not seen me – a voice crying in the wilderness.

Patton's high profile was exploited in his second role, that of commander of FUSAG (First United States Army Group), a fictitious army stationed at Dover. This army would, so the misinformation fed to the Germans said, be invading France through the Pas-de-Calais. (Another second, phantom army in Scotland created the impression of preparations for an invasion through Norway.)

Patton acted out his part as commander of FUSAG, touring bases in the south east of England. Dummy vehicles and landing craft were placed in likely embarkation points to fool German reconnaissance aircraft. Fake radio traffic helped create the impression of a hive of activity.

T. Osborne was a 15-year-old boy seaman on the Royal Navy rescue tug *Assiduous*. In May 1944, as *Assiduous* was towing a Phoenix unit (part of the artificial harbour to be built off the Normandy coast) to Southampton, he saw evidence of FUSAG's success:

> En-route from London we stopped in Dover with our tow, which was a huge concrete block a full five storeys

tall. How it could float, and for what purpose it was to be used, we dare not think. While at Dover, a 40mm Bofors [gun] was installed on the top of the 'Thing'. Dover was absolutely crammed with small naval vessels.

We passed by huge camouflaged structures made only of canvas and wood. During the two days we were there, the Germans shelled Dover three times; one shell landed in the centre of the town. Poor Dover! This really was the front line. We could only travel at a speed of three knots while pulling the concrete monster, and we were hoping that no 'E' boats would spot us during the night while moving on to Southampton.

Invasion forces were building up elsewhere around the south coast. On Portland Bill, Wren Barbara Bruford could see:

The Chesil beach had by this time become a parking place for all the US tanks and motor transport which was assembling for embarkation. For days there were long lines of vehicles and crowds of bored, nervous, weary GIs standing about being fed coffee and doughnuts by American Red Cross girls – very smart and all with impeccable nylons. We, out on the Bill, had our last incident – a hit and run raider who dropped a land mine close to the watchroom, bringing down the aerial tower but fortunately not causing any injuries.

Sapper A.J. Lane was in the 263rd Field Company RE, which would be clearing the beaches:

That critical time was approaching fast, with our briefings, training, etc., becoming more specific, concentrated and specialised. We were now encountering for the first time exact replicas of the beach obstacles we would have to remove or destroy in order to make the necessary gaps in the stout coastal defences of the enemy.

Hedgehogs, Tetrahedrons, Element 'C' barriers, poles, mined ramps, ground mines, barbed wire entanglements etc., were some of the anti-tank, anti-vehicle, anti-craft and anti-personnel obstacles likely to be met with by assault engineers in early attacks – and we worked hard on these in training.

... Because of the tight security required for such a major operation, where surprise was all important, the spearhead troops with their dangerous knowledge had to be constrained within well-defined limits, orders and regulations. We were confined to allocated camp areas, with communication restricted to military members of our own group units.

... It was expected that for the real task, our first efforts would have to be directed towards blasting obstacles above and below sea water. A good deal of the time in our camp was therefore spent in making up the neat packages and parcels into ready-made waterproof charges. These were designed so as to be rapidly placed on the various obstacles for equally rapid demolition. (... many boxes of good old-fashioned Durex rubber goods were used – or misused – for the purpose of waterproofing igniter switches – the safety pins of which could be extracted within the stretched outer skin of the Durex covering. They were also used for the protection of wristwatches and other personal items. There was also no doubt that many were secreted away in reserve for purposes and moments more for love than for war.)

At the beginning of June, Major Rex was in Essex:

> The countryside to a depth of several miles around Belhus Park was given over to military camps and there were invasion units concentrated on common land within the London suburbs north of Victoria docks.
>
> ... A paraphernalia of invasion was parked outside the garden gates and front doors of the ordinary homes of England, and this other strength of Britain, was soon bringing out cups of tea and homemade cake for the troops. Girls rushed out offering sweets, 'Go on take two'. Mothers were suggesting to the lads, 'come inside and sit down a minute'. They brought out their morning papers for the soldiers.
>
> But more orders came along the lines; men sprang off their vehicles, motors were tuned up, tank engines roared, spitting out their thick fumes; the convoys were moving towards the docks.
>
> Kiddies were running alongside, waving, excited, and shouting 'Can I come?'
>
> The military machine was now filling the main streets and civilians in their thousands had a tremendous picture thrust under their very noses.
>
> They stared hard; they seemed suddenly to realise the significance of it all. Men bit on their pipes; they waved their hats ... Women paused, girls in their summer frocks and threw kisses, and errand boys rested their bikes against the pavement kerb stones to look on ... Policemen held up the normal traffic; bus passengers stood up, got out, others pushed their faces against the windows ... Cheers and frantic waving developed, everybody took up this great expression.

The soldiers grinned, some were still eating their breakfast, some were smoking, one or two were actually shaving, going along.

Columns of tanks and the medium guns seemed to make a great impression on the crowd … Ben and I were co-ordinating the entire sea lift at Tilbury docks. One or two landing ships (tank) would be ticklish stowage jobs, and we were undertaking these personally.

The quaysides were very soon humming with activity. REME were carrying out the final phase of waterproofing the motors, so that when the vehicles took their sea bath the other side, they would emerge on to the shore with engines running. Colour bars on the front mudguards denoted that the various stages had been checked up. Tanks could take a six foot plunge into the tide, lorries somewhere around five, and the little jeep, with its yards of exhaust piping, going 'sky-high' could do practically the same.

… The actual motors instruments and wiring were a mass of greyish dirty putty mixture; engines all but choked … Once ashore and established on land, certain vital parts had to be de-proofed immediately.

I had to give special care to a brigadier's wireless van, as he would be using it before landing.

We completed the main deck by literally lifting into position a last couple of jeeps.

Drivers set about securing vehicles with chains, after which I inspected the deck to satisfy myself that there was room for movement in case of air attack and fire.

… The trim of the ship was slightly affected, port and starboard weights were unequal, but the stowage of armour was like that; it would be adjusted. We tucked a couple of jeeps into the wings of the bow, then the ramp was raised and the great jaws closed.

Chains rattled as everything was secured. I checked up on fire precautions and jumped ashore as the craft moved away; another was ready to take her place.

...The hours sped by – eventide came; the 'sledgehammer' activity was cooling off as the sun bade us farewell.

... It was D-Day minus two.

We had supper with the captain of our craft, an American with whom we swapped experiences for an hour, enjoying a couple of oranges.

Then we slipped down a manhole, picked our way along a corridor – bodies were everywhere – but we found our hammocks.

... All the fighting vehicles and lorries around were loaded up to fixed scale, to be self-existing [self-supporting] for at least 48 hours, with fresh water in jerricans, petrol, rations, ammunition and stores; powerful enough to keep the invasion effort on its feet for that period.

... Meals were ample. I had another chat with the skipper. He had been in Indian seas, in the Far East and was on the Sicilian invasion, so we had some common ground for chatter.

'Say, what's this going to be like?' he exclaimed with a hand tucked inside his pale green blouse. I wondered.

Before having been given command of a landing craft, his only training was a two-month course in a navigation school.

He passed things off by saying that he couldn't get lost on the sea these days; one simply followed the leader.

Defence gunners were fussing over their ack-ack [anti-aircraft] guns, and fondling belts of ammunition, getting that feeling of readiness for anything which might happen.

I went to bed about midnight. Sleep didn't come for a couple of hours. I wasn't tired and my mind was racing here, there and everywhere; if we might only switch off our mental activities, like the electric light near me …

'Blockships' were craft which were deliberately sunk to be part of a 'gooseberry'– an artificial harbour made from ships scuttled off each of the landing beaches. A.J. Holladay was a Royal Artillery subaltern in command of a troop attached to 114 LAA Regiment. He was on the *Empire Bunting,* a 6,300-ton cargo ship which was sent over to France to be sunk as a blockship. *Empire Bunting's* journey to France began at the Firth of Lorn on the west coast of Scotland on 31 May, and A.J. Holladay wrote about the slow and hazardous journey in his diary:

0830 We move off at last: Wren in launch waves us goodbye and good luck. Out of anchorage convoy forms into two columns. Practically at standstill for long while. Last view of Oban and Ben Cruachan. Move off through firth and form four columns. American convoy of Liberty ships form up behind. *Durban* comes up to lead our convoy. Escorts are Canadian frigate, corvettes and armed trawlers.

1100 Deterioration of weather. Breeze, rougher sea, sky overcast.

1400 Reach mouth of firth off Ross of Mull. Moderate swell from Atlantic. Steering gear breaks down: we avoid hitting *Panos* and lie wallowing clear of convoy. Escort

> vessels rush round us worrying to know what trouble is. Admiralty tug stands by.

The following day:

> 0300 Wakened by ship siren, shouts of alarm, and finally signal to abandon ship. Moment of internal panic. Emerge on deck in lifebelt to find ED *(Empire Defiance)* broadside on. Just missed a full-blooded ramming amidships which would have sunk us like a stone. Back to bed. (Our starboard light was out.)

Wren Shirley Gadsby was stationed on the south coast, conveniently near to her home:

> We were confined to barracks for at least a month before [D-Day], as were the local civilians who were not allowed to travel – was it not more than five miles, or ten? ... All the local lanes and fields filled up with troops and tanks rumbled through Fareham right under our windows. It was hard to sleep after 24 hours on, so I used to hop on a bus in civvies and go home to bed! When even the bus stopped, I used to bicycle home an illegal distance through the back lanes, and through whistling collections of soldiers … even if you had been dropped from Mars that day you would have known that something very big was about to happen. The sight of the whole of Portsmouth Harbour, Spithead, in fact all the water usually to be seen from up on the Portsdown Hills, was utterly invisible, covered so thickly with ships it was impossible to see any space between them.

At the end of May, Austin Baker was sent to a concentration area at Hursley Park, 6 miles east of Romsey, Hampshire:

> The camp was packed with troops and equipment of all kinds – tanks, self-propelled guns, … tank-busters, mobile Bofors, Bren carriers and infantry. The whole place was very well run by an American permanent staff. The food was much better than we had been used to for a very long time, and there were good NAAFIs [canteens] and several cinemas. We all slept in tents.
>
> We had nothing to do except seal the ARV ready for the landing – filling every hole and crack with bostik [for waterproofing] and fitting long, self-sealing chutes to the exhaust and air intake.
>
> The day before we were due to move we were given our briefing, though we were not told where we were actually going. We knew more or less what the beach looked like, and we knew that we had to make for an orchard near a little village a short distance inland, where the fitters and the first vehicles of A1 Echelon transport were to rendezvous …
>
> We were expecting to move at about midnight on June 2nd. We packed up our kit and stowed it away on the ARV, then we sat on our beds and waited for our serial number to be called over the loudspeaker system. At about midnight an announcement came over to the effect that our serial would be delayed for at least 2 hours. We had a little sleep, and at two o'clock we heard that there would be another two hours' delay. We had already had one late supper, but we went along to the mess room and scrounged another to pass the time.

> We finally moved off … soon after dawn on June 3rd.
>
> We rolled through Southampton and down to the docks, and we were loaded on to [a tank landing craft] with surprisingly little delay.
>
> The LCT was absolutely jammed with vehicles and guns and men. In addition to the ARV there was Major Barker's tank, the Intelligence Officer's tank, one A Squadron tank, Capt. Collins' scout car, a bulldozer, a jeep and three carriers towing 6 pounder anti-tank guns belonging to the Green Howards.

Coded messages broadcast on the BBC warned the French Resistance that the invasion was imminent so they could sabotage enemy transport and communications. The Germans usually responded to acts of sabotage with reprisals, murdering civilians.

Geneviève Duboscq was a 12-year-old girl living with her parents and younger brother a few miles from Sainte-Mère-Eglise on the Normandy coast. She wrote after the war about the family's experiences, including a journey with her mother, on 5 June. Upon seeing an exposed telephone cable running alongside the country road on which they are walking, her mother said:

> 'If I really thought that the invasion everyone is talking about were coming, I'd cut that cable. Then the Germans in Sainte-Mère would be cut off from their friends in Pont l'Abbé … Mama kept eyeing that telephone cable, which sometimes lay openly on the grass verge.
>
> 'I'll never forgive myself for not bringing the wire-cutters,' she muttered. 'It would be so easy to cut that cable.'

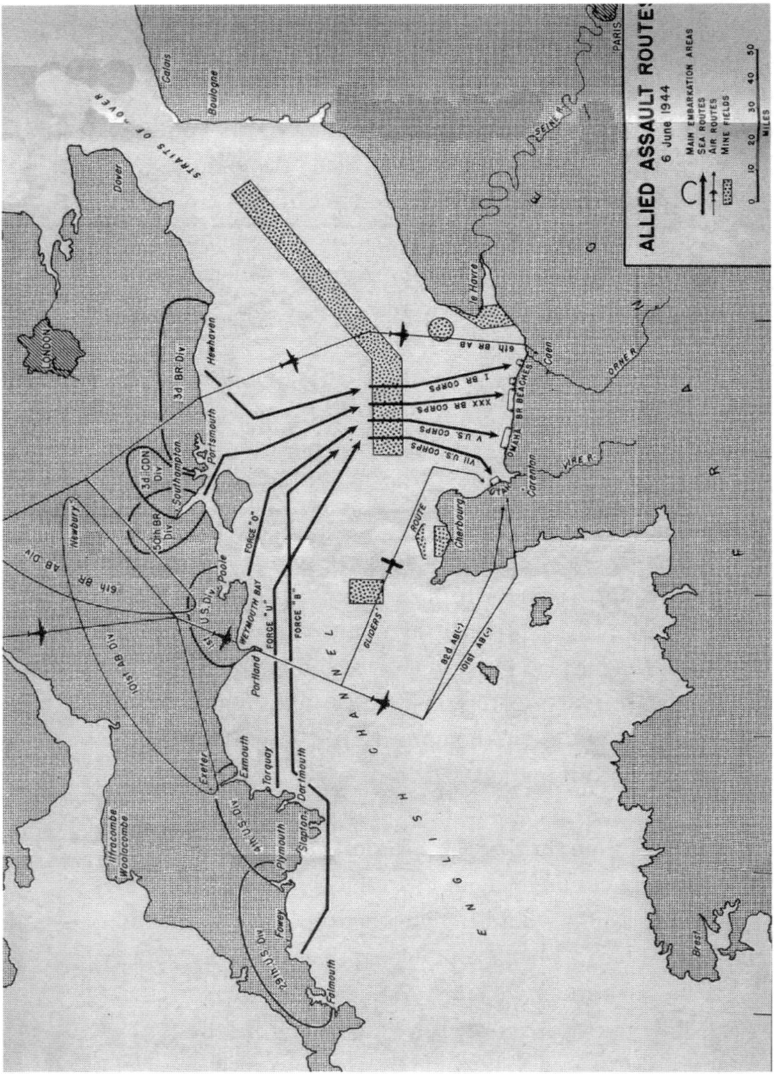

The route taken by the invading forces across the English Channel to Normandy. (Crown Copyright)

Geneviève borrowed some wirecutters from a nearby house.

> With one quick snip, Mama had cut the cable. Then she stood up and walked a few steps down the road, motioning me to follow. Again we sat down by the ditch. Again she cut the cable, and I took the loose piece and flung it behind a hedge.
>
> It was our first act of sabotage – but it wasn't over yet. Mama hid the wire-cutters under the dandelion leaves in the basket and we strolled innocently down the road for a hundred yards or so. Again we sat down at the edge of the ditch, and repeated the operation. Mama had decided that we should make a dozen or more cuts, every few yards, so that the Germans would not be able to repair the cable simply by pulling and splicing it together. This way they would have to replace the entire length …
>
> By the time we arrived home we were both shivering. As we trudged the last few yards to the house, Mama glanced out over the greenish waters of the swamp, lapping at the embankment by the level-crossing.
>
> 'If the Allies are coming,' she said, 'I hope they don't come by the sea.'

The intended date was the night of 4/5 June. However, at the last minute, the weather in the Channel deteriorated and it was called off.

Wren Gwyneth Verdon-Roe, a plotter at Dartmouth, tracking ships in and out of the Channel, wrote to her mother shortly afterwards:

> The night of the 4th/5th June, I was on all night. We worked flat out until dawn and then the whole thing was

called off because of the weather. The disappointment was terrible, the anti-climax after all the stress. We were tearful and tired and had never felt so low in all our lives … Have any of my letters been cut to shreds by the censor? It is difficult because I can read in the papers things that would be censored in a letter.

The longer the Allies delayed, the greater the risk that the invasion plans would be discovered by the Germans. The invasion could be launched on only a few days each month, when the moon was full and the spring tides were favourable – and provided the weather was good enough to enable the invaders to cross the sea and land in France, ready to fight their way off the beaches.

3

Airborne Assault

Airborne troops from the Allied forces, arriving by glider and by parachute, were the prelude to the landings on the beaches of Normandy. They were to capture key positions and defend the troops coming in from the sea from German counter-attacks.

Over 24,000 troops from the British, Canadian, Free French and US forces began landing in France shortly after midnight on 6 June.

It was the largest ever use of airborne troops: two US airborne divisions – the 82nd and 101st – and the British 6th Airborne Division were to secure the beachheads on the eastern and western flanks.

British airborne

The British 6th Airborne Division's target was to the north-east of Caen. The division was to prevent the Germans sending armoured units to attack the left flank of Sword Beach. To do this, it had to capture and hold the bridges the Allies would need to take the invasion on to the city of Caen. It also had to destroy a German gun battery at Merville and bridges to the east over the River Dives. The division was to then hold a line between the Caen Canal and the River Orne until it linked with advancing Allied ground troops.

Jim Wallwork was a pilot in the Glider Pilot Regiment, which was formed in 1942. The pilots were recruited from the army and trained by the RAF, as Wallwork wrote after the war:

> In early March 1944 six glider crews were collected at Netheravon from various flights of the regiment. No word as to why, in the usual glider pilot style, but we foregathered at mid-field and were addressed by our colonel, George Chatterton, behind whom appeared a convoy of army and air force brass ... He pointed out a couple of triangles marked with broad white tape, one here, one there on the airfield. Not very big, but apparently in his judgement, big enough.
>
> Briefing was very succinct: 'You will be towed at one-minute intervals to 4,000ft, which will take about one hour. You will then release three miles away at a point decided by your tug, from where you will be able to see these triangles. Numbers 1, 2 and 3 will land in this one, making a right hand circuit, and 4, 5 and 6 on t'other from a left hand circuit. Now hop off for lunch. All gliders are ready and assembled on the towpath. Take off 1300hrs.'
>
> No word as to how we were chosen. Perhaps drawn from a hat? Perhaps crews of our squadron commanders were glad to part with? We were all sergeants. My co-pilot was Johnnie Ainsworth. I was told to fly first and, although throughout training the other crews changed numbers and patterns (a wise move), I always stayed as number 1. So we took off and flew a short course, saw the triangles, cast off and landed all six in our correct areas, to our utter astonishment. A mutter of disbelief emanated from the

brass, and a few low-key bragging words about 'his boys' from George.

... From that point, the operation was 'on' although no-one mentioned it to us. And Deadstick, the codename for the glider pilot training, started. Vice-Marshal Arthur Harris, Chief of the Air Staff, [said] that it would be disastrous to try to train army personnel to fly troop-carrying gliders. His actual words were: 'The idea that semi-skilled, unpicked personnel ... could, with a maximum of training, be entrusted with the piloting of these troop carriers is fantastic. Their operation is equivalent to forced landing the largest sized aircraft without engine aid – that which there is no higher test of piloting skill.' We can now extend a belated thank you to Bomber Harris as he became known, for such an accolade to the Glider Pilot Regiment ...

The first battle of D-Day took place just after midnight on 6 June, when glider-borne troops from the 2nd Battalion Oxfordshire and Buckinghamshire Light Infantry, led by Major John Howard, landed in Normandy. They were to capture two bridges: over the Caen Canal near the village of Bénouville, and over the River Orne, ¼ mile away, at the village of Ranville.

Jim Wallwork remembered:

At last we were told where, how, and why the two bridges over the River Orne and Caen Canal had to be taken intact and held. Gliders 1–3, flying the three course path, we were to take the canal, while 4–6 would drop straight down and take the river... we took off at 22.45 through low cloud and into clear sky at 6,000ft over the channel.

> It was a smooth flight and Howard encouraged the men to sing; none were airsick. Thanks to our tug crew we were dead on time and dead on target. 'Cast Off', the singing stopped and that was when six Horsas tiptoed quietly into two little fields in Normandy and released 180 fighting men in full battle order to give the German garrison the surprise of their lives …
>
> … I hit the field and caught the first bit of wire and so I called 'Stream', and by golly it [the parachute] lifted the tail and forced the nose down. It drew us back and knocked the speed down tremendously. It was only on for two seconds, and 'jettison,' and Ainsworth pressed the tit and jettisoned the parachute, and then we were going along only about 60 [mph], which was ample to take me, right into the corner. We got right into the corner of the field, the nose wheel had gone, the cockpit collapsed, and Ainsworth and I went right through the cockpit. I went overhead first and landed flat on my stomach. I was stunned, as was Ainsworth; I came around and he seemed to be in bad shape. I said, 'Can you crawl?' and he said, 'No,' and then I asked if I lifted, could he crawl out and he said, 'I'll try.' I lifted the thing and I felt that I lifted the whole bloody glider when probably all I lifted was a small spar, but I felt like 30 men when I picked this thing up and he did manage to crawl out.

Jim Wallwork landed No 1 glider shortly after midnight near the Bénouville Bridge over the Caen Canal. Those on board were the first Allied troops to set foot in France on D-Day.

> Although we made an awful noise on landing we seemed not to bother the German sentries. I was stunned and

pinned under the collapsed cockpit, but the troops were getting on with it. Exactly one minute later No.2 arrived and joined in, followed by No. 3 – this all justified those training flights. Long afterwards we all confessed to feeling rather pleased with ourselves at having pulled it off, this when June 6 was 20 minutes old and our little battle was just starting. Air Chief Marshall Leigh-Mallory called it the greatest flying feat of the Second World War.

There was only one casualty on landing, the Bren gunner in No. 3 who drowned in a pond. Johnnie and I revived in a few minutes and with the aid of a medic I crawled free of the debris. I made myself useful carting ammunition from the glider to the troops, then we heard a Tank. We needed Gammon anti-tank bombs, but I could not find those bloody bombs, so took a case of 303 which made Howard cross. 'Get the bloody Gammons,' he hollered.

It was a rough night. We pilots did what little we could to help but when the Parachute Brigade arrived at 0300hrs and Lord Lovat at about 1300hrs on the 6th, they were indeed welcome. By daylight my legs had seized and I became a stretcher case and after local medical assistance ended up at Ronkswood Hospital in Worcester.

Harry 'Nobby' Clarke was in the second of the three gliders to land near the Bénouville Bridge. He had joined D Company of the 2nd Battalion Oxfordshire and Buckinghamshire Light Infantry in the early months of 1942.

Major John Howard turned out to be a very hard and tough taskmaster, with expectation of the highest standards from those he commanded. He was the boss.

But his training routine produced a company that was second to none in the British Army. Our main mode of transport was army boots. In other words, we marched everywhere. If you did not make the grade, 'D' company was not good for your health.

... On the 2nd May 1944, the company assembled in 22 platoon room to listen to a talk by Major Howard. Firstly we were sworn to a vow of secrecy ... Our task in the invasion of Europe was to capture bridges at night. That the re-entry into Europe was to happen very soon, within weeks. There was to be a period of special training starting that very day after the meeting. From that moment in time bridges took full control of our very lives. In the next few weeks we captured many make-believe bridges. We ate, drank and dreamt about bridges. The powers that be located two bridges in Devon. They were very similar to the bridges we were training to capture intact. We then moved to the Exeter region and spent three days and nights of intensive training on these two bridges. Our very lives depended on the practice ...

... We were dead certain that if the gliders put us down in the right position we could take our bridge. But the question of holding it against strong enemy tank counter-attacks was going to be a problem. The major's reply to this was 'We must hold them', so that answered the question. It was now just a question of waiting for the weather to improve. Each Horsa Glider would carry 2 pilots, 5 Royal Engineers, 23 airborne infantry: 30 men altogether. Six Horsas were to land a total of 180 men in total ...

... They set off on the night of the 5th June.

Landing ships putting cargo ashore during the first days of the invasion (Archives Normandie 1939–1945)

It was just a short run to Tarrant Rushton Airfield. As we passed the admin area, crowds of RAF men and women were cheering us. So much for security, everyone knows what we are about to do. It did very little for my morale.

> We drove direct to our six Horsa gliders and sat down on the grass beside them. The time was about 2200hrs.
>
> … Horsa glider No.91 carried 24 platoon commanded by Lt David Wood, mainly young men going into action

for the first time. Tonight would be a testing time. But I had trained with those men over the last two years and had no doubts as to their ability.

Inside the glider the men sat in a strained silence. For all in 24 it was their first night flight, apart of course from the two pilots who had done much night flying in training for this operation ...

Just after midnight on 6 June, they neared their target:

The silence was broken by the sound of air rushing across the huge wings of the Horsa glider as it [sped] towards its landing. A sudden shout from one of the glider pilots, 'Brace for impact': we linked our hands and raised our feet and no doubt said a silent prayer. The Horsa hit the ground and bushes and then stopped, but the passengers were propelled through either the side of the Horsa or the open front exit. We very swiftly formed up at the nose of the Horsa and at a word of command from Lt Wood began to trot towards the bridge some one hundred or so yards to our front.

As we reached the eastern end of the bridge, a flare lit up the area. Some thirty or so yards from the bridge lay the wreck of a Horsa, its two pilots trapped in its cockpit. By the light of the flare we could see our troops running across the canal bridge, firing as they ran. Lt Wood located Major Howard who ordered our platoon to clear the enemy from the pillbox and trenches on the North Eastern bank of the canal.

We very swiftly complied with this order, helped by some of the enemy who ran away and hid in the bushes. In perhaps six or seven minutes, we routed the enemy.

> Lt Wood was on his way to Major Howard to report all cleared when he, the platoon sergeant and radio operator were hit by a burst of automatic fire. Corporal Godbold reported to John Howard who gave him command of the platoon and he in turn gave the 38 type radio set to me. We had captured our bridge ...

Over the Orne River bridge, one of the three gliders landed 8 miles east of the targer, over the River Dives. Troops from the other two gliders captured the bridge, which was defended by a machine-gun nest.

Nobby Clarke recalled:

> The bridge defence system had been overrun in a matter of minutes. All opposition crushed and the three platoons were now in a position of all round defence by 00:45. The 3rd and 5th Parachute Brigades were to begin their drop at 00:50. Right on time we heard the roar of hundreds of aircraft engines and streams of fire from enemy anti-aircraft guns lit up the night sky.
>
> Flares were fired and it was wonderful to see the hundreds of parachutes dropping to the east of the river bridge. A company of the 7th Parachute Battalion was due to hurry to reinforce our tiny force holding the two bridges.
>
> In Bénouville village, at around 02:00GMT, the sound of enemy tanks sent a shiver down the spines of the defenders. Whilst we were happy to do battle against infantry, tanks were a different kettle of fish.
>
> Whatever happened that night the enemy must be denied the opportunity of recapturing the two bridges. We mustered the few PIAT's [anti-tank weapons] still available

and set up a string of Hawkins Grenades in preparation to pull across the road. A platoon of the river bridge defenders was rushed over to the Bénouville west bank. The road leading to the hamlet of le Port was covered. A PIAT carried by Sgt Thornton was hastily rushed up to cover the road junction. Several tanks were approaching this junction, followed by a number of infantry. The expected counterattack was about to materialise right on time. As the leading tank nosed up to the road junction a well-directed shot from seventeen platoon's Sgt Thornton set the tank on fire and as the shells, small-arms ammunition and flares began to explode the enemy force withdrew in some haste. Thanks to the good aim of Sgt Thornton we had won a respite from what could have turned into a serious situation. Back on the canal bridge Cpl Ted Tappenden was still sending out the success signal, HAM and JAM, HAM and JAM, constantly broadcast via his 38 wireless set, and Major Howard was blasting out the V for Victory signal on his whistle, to guide the expected 7th Para. While all this action was taking place I had been on a watching patrol with Cpl Godbold. He had moved the section commanded by L/Cpl Roberts into a position on the west side of the canal facing in the direction of Le Port. The body of an elderly man clad in a long nightshirt lay in the front garden of the building on the north side of the road opposite the cafe. The platoon was down in number to just 20 men. One section area reported possible movement to their immediate front. We knew that several enemy troops had run off in that direction during our initial attack. The corporal suggested that the two of us should do a short reconnaissance along the towpath in a coastal direction. This turned out to be a rather nerve-racking experience. The moon was bright and every bush and tree was a possible enemy position. After some 150 or so yards we took cover in a clump of bushes and watched for any sign or sound of movement to our front. Some 15 or 20 minutes later all being quiet we rejoined the platoon. Giving our call designation Baker-Baker as the password we entered the platoon area and took up a position with our backs against the large German pillbox close to the canal bridge. The noise emanating from the burning tank gave the impression that a full-scale battle was raging in the area of the crossroads. The screams of one of the tankmen who had been trapped in the vehicle had done little for our nerves. Whilst watching in the direction of Le Port we noted a fair amount of movement, it was difficult to make out who they were so we decided to leave them well alone as long as they stayed where they were.

As a village clock chimed 2 a.m. shadowy figures began crossing the canal bridge, the first arrivals from the 7th Parachute Battalion were moving into Bénouville, it was a great feeling to know that we had been reinforced.

Tim Roseveare commanded the 3rd Parachute Squadron RE. He was responsible for linking with the 8th Parachute Battalion and destroying the five bridges across the River Dives. The troops landed several miles from their objective, but by 2.30 a.m. on 6 June Roseveare had gathered as many men and as much equipment as he could. Commandeering a Jeep, he set off for one of the bridges, at Troarn:

We had set off down the road at a moderate pace with everyone ready with a Bren gun or one of our several

> Sten guns for any trouble. Just before the level crossing we ran slap into a barbed wire knife-rest road block. One Boche fired a shot and then went off. It took twenty minutes hard work with wire cutters before the jeep was freed. We then proceeded on, leaving behind, it transpired later, Sapper Moon; two scouts were sent ahead to the next crossroads.

The two scouts found a lone German sentry:

> On being dragged from his bicycle he protested volubly and we made the mistake of silencing him with a Sten gun instead of a knife. The town was now getting roused so we lost no time and everyone jumped aboard while I tried to make the best speed possible. As the total load was 3000lbs we only made about 35mph. At the corner the fun started. There seemed to be a Boche in every doorway shooting like mad. However, the boys got to work with their Sten guns and Sapper Peachey did very good work as rear gunner with the Bren gun. What saved the day was the steep hill down the main street. As the speed rose rapidly and we careered from side to side of the road, – the heavy trailer was swinging violently, we were chased out of the town by a German machine gun which fired tracer just over our heads.

Sapper Peachey was thrown out in the descent and taken prisoner. The rest found the bridge that they had come to destroy unguarded and, five minutes later, blew a gap of nearly 20ft in the centre.

The parachutists were widely scattered, and most of their radios and heavy weapons had been lost. Some met up with British troops at the Caen and Orne bridges, and defended the bridges against uncoordinated but fierce German counter-attacks throughout D-Day. At 7 p.m. on 6 June, the British 3rd Infantry Division arrived to relieve the airborne troops.

Later, the bridge over the Caen Canal was renamed Pegasus Bridge in honour of the British airborne forces, whose shoulder emblem is the flying horse Pegasus. The bridge over the River Orne was renamed Horsa Bridge, after the gliders that brought the Allied forces.

A fortnight after landing in France, Captain C.T. Cross, a platoon commander inthe 2nd Battalion Oxfordshire & Buckinghamshire Light Infantry, wrote home about his experiences on 6 June:

> 23 June, 1944
> I have just changed my underclothes and washed my feet for the first time since I left England … What we would really like is some bread – getting awfully tired of these biscuits, but the army bakers are not here yet and the local French don't have any to spare …
>
> The glider flight was bloody! It was, of course, longer than most we've done before because of the business of getting into formation, collecting fighter escort and so on. After about ¼ hour I began to be sick and continued until we were over the Channel where the air was much calmer.
>
> The Channel was a wonderful sight – especially the traffic at this end – Piccadilly Circus wasn't in it. We were not over the coast this side long enough for me to be sick again and we were pretty busy thinking about landing. The landing was ghastly.

Mine was the first glider down though we were not quite in the right place, and the damn thing bucketed along a very upsy-downsy field for a bit and then broke across the middle – we just chopped through those anti-landing poles (like the ones I used to cut during my forestry vac [vacation]) as we went along. However the two halves of the glider fetched up very close together and we quickly got out ourselves, and our equipment, and lay down under the thing because other gliders were coming in all round, and Jerries were shooting about at them, and us, so it wasn't very healthy to wander about.

Our immediate opposition – a machine gun in a little trench – was very effectively silenced by another glider which fetched up plumb on the trench and a couple of Huns – quite terrified – came out with their hands up! Having discovered that we were all there and bound up a few scratches we then set off to the scene of the battle. I shall not tell you about that except that apart from a bar of chocolate and half the contents of my whiskey flask, I had no time to eat or drink for a very uncomfortably long time – too much else to do, but it seems incredible now. From my last meal in England to my first cup of char and hard ration in France was very nearly 48 hours! But I've been making up for it since.

Somebody once said that war was composed of intensive boredom relieved by periods of acute fear. That is it in a nutshell. The boys used to hate digging themselves trenches on Salisbury Plain but you should just see how fast they do it now! And we've had a good many to dig in various different places since we came here. My hands are not what they were.

US Airborne

In the early hours of 6 June, US paratroopers of the 82nd and 101st Airborne Divisions landed on the Cotentin Peninsula, the westernmost edge of the invasion area. They were to stop German forces from attacking US troops as they landed on Utah beach.

The 82nd Airborne Division was to take control of two rivers: the Douve, by destroying key bridges, and the Mederet by taking control of both banks. The division was also to capture the German garrison stationed at the town of Sainte-Mère-Eglise, which was on the road between the town of Carentan and the port of Cherbourg.

The US 101st Airborne Division was to secure exits from Utah beach, for the invading US infantry, destroy bridges over the River Douve and a German coastal battery, and capture the lock at the village of La Barquette.

The 13,000 US parachute troops were to be dropped in hundreds of C-47 aircraft, each plane carrying a 'stick' of eighteen parachutists. As they crossed the Channel on the night of 5/6 June, the weather was clear until just before the French coast, when the planes were scattered in a thick bank of cloud over the target area. Markers were lost and the planes came under fire from German artillery.

Colonel Charles Young was a pilot, the commanding officer of the 439th Troop Carrier Group. Colonel Young reached Normandy at 1.08 a.m. on 6 June and wrote shortly after in his diary:

> I began to recognize some of the features of the landscape and knew where we were. Our navigators confirmed that

we were on course, and soon I could see the pattern of the flooded areas in the reflected moonlight which was filtering through the clouds somewhat. By the time we were halfway across the peninsula, I picked out the road that ran through the north part of our assigned drop zone, DZ 'C'. I made a slight course correction to the right, and we went directly over the DZ, which was located about three miles southeast of Sainte-Mère-Eglise, three miles west of the east coastline and close to Sainte-Marie-du-Mont and north of Hiesville.

We had been receiving some fire, evidently from machine guns and some heavier flak from the time we had crossed the west coast. As we were approaching the DZ machine-gun fire and flak began increasing, and a ship in our 45-ship serial, flown by 2nd Lt Marsten Sargent, was shot down. The intense flames from the gasoline fire lit up the lower cloud layer above us and gave an eerie orange-yellow cast to the formation and to the scene below us.

Machine-gun fire with yellow tracers came from the right rear where we crossed the railroad that ran from Cherbourg to Carentan. The tracers went by the nose of my ship so thick at this point that they lit up the inside of the cockpit. Later I found out that much of my No.2 element had been shot up, though none were shot down by this fire. Tracers of various colors – red, green, blue, and orange – came from guns two to three miles from the north in a head converging on our column and by now tracers were crossing in front of us and around us, and large explosions were occurring along the coastline ahead of us. The combination of these several guns shot down two more ships of our second serial of 36 ships, led by Major Tower. The two that crashed were flown by Lt Harold Capelluto and Lt Marvin Muir. Lt Muir was able to hold his plane in the air long enough to jump their stick of troopers, and he and his crew sacrificed their own lives to do so.

After our troopers were dropped and the area cleared, we turned north-eastward to cross the Saint-Marcouf Islands. North of the islands I got up and looked back through the astrodome to check on the formation. Tracers were coming from a point about six miles behind us, up through and among us in a huge, snake-like arc, so I climbed back into my seat with some speed where I had a little protection from some armor-plate I'd had installed there.

Passing Cherbourg, well offshore, shells started lobbing out at a point ahead and getting nearer our course with each shot. I veered slightly to the far side of the course to make it more sporting.

As we intercepted the course that we had taken from the Bill of Portland, on the way in, other formations could still be seen going in, as the airborne train was several hundred miles long. I called those formations – breaking radio silence for what I was certain now to be an emergency – and told them to hit the coast at 700 feet instead of 1,500 feet.

First Lieutenant Neal Beaver, of the 508th Parachute Infantry Regiment, recalled his journey to France in correspondence with Robert Nelson, Flight Leader with the 29th Troop Carrier Squadron, 313th Troop Carrier Group, which was carrying Beaver and other US parachutists to Normandy that night.

> We were so loaded up with ammo, guns, mines, demolition packs, rations etc., that we must have weighed 300 pounds each. How those fantastic C-47s got off the ground that night is still a mystery to me. As I recall, it was a worry to the aircrew also because I can remember much fussing and discussing over that center of gravity calculator that night. Since we were all young and ignorant, I assume your guys finally just said: the hell with it; it will probably fly! I do recall that our angle of ascent was so flat that it is fortunate that the tall TV antennas were in the future.

Their flight of three aircraft took off late and so they arrived over the target in Normandy alone. As the plane neared the drop zone:

> ...we came under machine-gun fire. The first burst looked like it was coming straight for my forehead, but it swept by in a gentle curve to the east.
>
> The next burst caught us front to rear. The plane took a sudden lurch, lost some more altitude, and roared back up to speed. Nelson had evidently set up for the 'Go' light as soon as he completed the turn. I found out later that he and some others of the crew had been wounded. This first burst nicked Bill Gary across the nose, and I caught a 9mm round in the jaw. It knocked me back, but I bounced back into the door and as the green light snapped on, I kept right on going out of the plane.
>
> As it turned out, the full bore jump saved us because our chutes snapped open with such speed. I know I oscillated just once or twice and hit the ground hard.
>
> Your guys did a great job, considering the circumstances. Three planes, alone, out over the opposite shore and then

directly into a flurry of flak and fire, yet the three planes stayed so tight. I had my entire platoon of 50+ troopers all together by 6:00 that morning. (I hit the ground at 1:30am.)

As part of the defences, the area had been flooded by the enemy; many of the troops dropped on the Cotentin Peninsula drowned in the marshes and most of the equipment was lost. The wide dispersal of the parachute troops confused and hindered US attempts to join up. It also confused the German military commanders, whose response was further hampered by the absence of senior officers, most of whom were away on a training exercise. The French Resistance, forewarned in coded messages broadcast to secret radios and by the BBC World Service, cut telephone lines, preventing the Germans from assessing the extent of the invasion.

In their home three miles from Sainte-Mère-Eglise, Geneviève Duboscq's family decided to celebrate the start of the invasion:

Papa told me to set some glasses on the table while he went down to the cellar to fetch the cider … He turned to go down the cellar, but before he had taken two steps the kitchen door was suddenly kicked open from outside, and standing framed against the darkness was a strangely dressed man carrying a machine gun, which was aimed menacingly at us.

… He kicked the door shut behind him, as violently as he had kicked it open; he didn't say a word. He just kept looking at us, as though waiting for someone to make a wrong move. My heart was pounding; I sensed, in that frozen moment, that if any of us did move he would surely kill us on the spot ...

Finally the stranger broke the silence. 'Friend or foe?' he asked, in perfect French.

'What a silly question,' I thought; as if anyone would ever answer 'Foe!' Anyway, how could he possibly think we were enemies, we who had been waiting for five long years for the Allies to come? ...
It was Claude [her brother] who finally answered him. 'Friends, Monsieur – we're all friends.' His high little voice echoed round the room as he walked straight up to the soldier, his hands stretching towards the barrel of the machine gun.

'Friends,' the soldier repeated, lowering the gun at last. 'Really friends?' And he ran his grimy hand through Claude's blond hair.

We all breathed again. Following my little brother's example, I went over to the soldier and kissed him on the cheek. He looked surprised, but pleased. The whole room now relaxed, and my parents came back to life and walked over to him.

The soldier pulled a map from his pocket and laid it out on the table.

'Show me where the Germans are' he said, indicating his map.

It was the first time Papa Maurice had ever seen a military map but he seemed at ease. He leant over the table and studied it for a moment, then he lifted his head and asked the soldier: 'Where is my house on the map?'

The soldier pointed to a little black square. Then, with a little grey stub of a pencil that the soldier lent him, Papa underlined several places.

'The Germans are here, at the Château d'Amfreville,' he said, 'about a mile from here. And at Port-de-Neuville, also about a mile away. At Fresville, too – that's just over a mile from here. And they're at the Château de La Fière, too; that's also about one mile away.'

'You mean we're surrounded,' said the soldier.

Papa Maurice looked surprised. 'We?' he said. 'What do you mean – "we"? You're not alone?'

'No, of course not,' the soldier grinned. 'Hear all those planes? They're full of paratroopers who are being dropped in.'

Mama, who had gone very pale, I noticed, moved over to him. 'You mean, Monsieur, that lots of paratroopers are going to come down here tonight?'

'Not, "going to come", Madame,' he said. 'They're coming down right this minute.'

'But they can't!' she cried. 'You've got to stop them – quick before it's too late. They'll all drown!' And she seized his arm and led him to the level-crossing gate. The marsh waters were washing against the embankment only a yard away. 'You've got to stop them,' she repeated. 'They'll all be killed if they land here.'

The soldier turned to Papa. 'How deep is that water?'

'Four or five feet,' Papa told him. 'Almost six feet in some places. But that's not the worst of it. The River Merderet flows through the swamp, and of course the water's much deeper there.'

More confusion was caused when dummy paratroopers were dropped west of Saint-Lô by American forces, and Field Marshal Rommel ordered all reinforcements to what he thought was another seaborne invasion.

German soldiers in Normandy tried to make sense of events. Lieutenant Ulrich Radermann was a paratrooper stationed near Rennes:

> On the morning of 6 June I was ordered to report to General Meindl, our CO of 5th Parachute Division, and go to 84th Corps and find out what the situation was as we were completely in the dark. We knew only that enemy airborne troops had landed. We had received no orders and it was all very unsatisfactory. Communications were proving difficult owing to air attack and a certain amount of Resistance sabotage. So I selected a Sergeant I knew as very reliable. We had a motorcycle combination and knew the best route to travel.
>
> When we reached 84th Corps HQ [at St Lô] we found panic and a complete lack of decision-making. I did not know what to make of it, and when I tried to telephone my own HQ at Rennes and speak to General Meindl it proved impossible to get through. I decided all I could do was try to investigate the situation for myself. It was still quite early, about nine o'clock, when we set off north.
>
> We travelled fairly fast and soon ran into our army patrols who warned us of American parachutists in the area. The soldiers were trying to find them, but it was difficult owing to the woody nature of the countryside. So we rode on cautiously in a northerly direction until reaching a crossroads and a military policeman, who passed on the same warning of enemy paratroops. He was in a rather exposed position and looked very nervous. So on we went, still going north and feeling we now had a better idea of the situation. I decided to travel a few more miles to see if the troops in the beach-head were holding.

We almost reached a village a few miles from the sea when we heard shouts and bursts of automatic fire. Our motorcycle went out of control into the side of the road and we were flung off. I was dazed, but my Sergeant was hurt. We found ourselves prisoners of some Americans who had blackened faces and looked very fierce.

They removed our weapons and belts and took us to a little copse where we found an officer with another man who spoke some German. He said, 'You are paratroops like us?' I shrugged my shoulders and the officers asked us questions – where were we going, etc. I refused to answer, so they tied us up with some cords and we were given some whisky from a small flask. My Sergeant was badly bruised so I asked for medical attention, but the American officer said they had no doctor. Then most of the Americans left on patrol, leaving two men to guard us who were chewing and smoking, so I whispered to my Sergeant that we could try to escape, but then saw he was in no position to do anything of the sort. So he said, 'Lieutenant, it is your duty to get away if you can. Don't worry – I'll survive!'

He was right, so I pretended to fall asleep. And at the right moment, as the two Americans strolled away, I leapt up and ran off as fast as I could with my hands tied. The guards ran after me, shouting and shooting, but I had the advantage. I ran like mad through the trees, leapt over several ditches and went under hedges until I reached a little road where I collapsed to rest and see if I had been followed. But no one came, so I got up and ran along the road, hoping it was the right direction. To my great joy I soon met one of our army patrols who untied me. I told them the location of the American paratroopers and they went off to look for them and try to rescue my

> Sergeant. One of their vehicles drove me back to their field headquarters which was of the 21st Panzer Division. From there I was able to get a message to my own HQ at Rennes, and by nightfall I reported to General Meindl. My Sergeant was not recovered, but remained a PoW [prisoner of war]. I met him again after the war.

Twenty-six trunk telephone lines were cut on D-Day, including the lines between the towns of Saint-Lô and of Avranches, and the cities of Cherbourg and Caen. Other acts of sabotage, many of them planned for months by the French Resistance and the Allies, resulted in major disruption to roads and railways, and prevented the German forces in the area from linking up effectively.

At Sainte-Mère-Eglise, many US parachutists were killed as they dropped directly on to the village, the sky lit up by flames from a burning building. Those who landed were taken prisoner, after which their German captors went back to bed. As dawn broke on 6 June, Lieutenant Colonel Ed Krause, commander of US 3rd Battalion, 505th Parachute Infantry Regiment, arrived with 180 parachutists. A villager showed him where the Germans were sleeping; thirty were captured, ten killed and some escaped. It was the first town to be liberated by the invading Allied forces.

Most of the objectives of the US airborne assault had not been secured as the invasion force began to arrive on Utah beach. The American landings were therefore vulnerable to attack, but the widespread dispersal of the US paratroops continued to mislead the German military commanders. They believed the US forces had occupied a wider area than was actually the case and were unable to launch an effective and co-ordinated counter-attack.

Even so, US airborne troops were unable to stop German anti-aircraft units from keeping up a barrage against the following gliders, which were bringing in reinforcements and heavy equipment. This, and the high hedgerows on the ground, were effective against the invading forces.

By midday on 6 June, however, men from the 101st Airborne had linked up with the US 4th Infantry division coming in from Utah Beach.

Many of the US airborne forces spent several days wandering the countryside, trying to link up. Casualties were high: 2,500 US airborne troops were killed or injured in the operation.

4

Across the Channel

On 4 June, at a meeting of the Supreme Headquarters Allied Expeditionary Force (SHAEF), Group Captain James Stagg, the chief meteorologist to Eisenhower, said that a brief improvement in the weather was likely the following night of 5/6 June. SHAEF commanders calculated the risk and, despite the problems in providing air cover, Eisenhower, his Chief of Staff General Walter Bedell Smith and Field Marshal Montgomery wanted to go ahead with the invasion. Admiral Bertram Ramsay, Naval Commander in Chief of the Allied Naval Expeditionary Force, thought conditions would be better, but Air Chief Marshal Leigh-Mallory was doubtful. The next day, Field Marshal Alanbrooke wrote:

> 5th June
> It is very hard to believe that in a few hours the cross Channel invasion starts! I am very uneasy about the whole operation. At the best it will fall so very, very far short of the expectation of the bulk of people, namely all those who know nothing of the difficulties. At the worst it may well be the most ghastly disaster of the whole war. I wish to God it were safely over.

Commenting later he said:

I knew too well all the weak points in the plan of the operations. First of all the weather, on which we were entirely dependent; a sudden storm might wreck it all. Then the complexity of an amphibious operation of this kind, when confusion may degenerate into chaos in such a short time. The difficulty of controlling the operation once launched, lack of elasticity in the handling of reserves, danger of leakage of information with consequent loss of that essential secrecy. Perhaps one of the most nerve-wracking experiences when watching an operation like this unroll itself is the intimate knowledge of the various commanders engaged. Too good a knowledge of their various weaknesses makes one wonder whether in the moments of crisis facing them they will shatter one's hopes.

To realise what it was like living through those agonising hours, the background of the last 3 years must be remembered. All those early setbacks, the gradual checking of the onrush, the very gradual turn of the defensive to the offensive, then that series of Mediterranean offensives alternately leading up to this final all important operation which started in the early hours of the next morning.

T. Osbourne recalled that on 5 June:

[the rescue tug *Assiduous*] … stood by in readiness for immediate duty off the Lee Tower in the Solent. At 9:00 our captain was taken ashore to attend a conference between the British and American naval officers and captains of merchant ships. The captain returned at 13:00 carrying a box. He was accompanied by an armed guard who looked quite fierce. When we saw the box, we knew it carried our orders for the invasion. At this moment,

I looked over the water to the Isle of Wight, with its green hills that looked so lovely in the distance and thought of a line from a Dylan Thomas poem: 'It is the green fuse that makes the flowers grow.'

The month of May means new life springing up everywhere, yet thousands of the boys and young men on the ships around me would never live to see another springtime.

The captain called us together and read a message from General Montgomery and General Eisenhower. He then asked God to keep us safe. I felt suspended in time and space, aware that this scene was being enacted on thousands of ships sitting in the sparkling seas along the English coast. We were given a Last Will and Testament form to sign. All crew members were then shown how to use the small tubes containing morphine! Lifejackets were inflated and lights tested. The crew was then dismissed.

An American tug, the USS *Partridge*, came alongside and because of my young age, I was given many chocolate bars and sweets by its crew. Their swear words were new to my ears and sounded awful; however, they were kind to me.

The night was noisy. At midnight, German pathfinder planes flew in through the clouds low over Portsmouth and dropped chandelier flares over the invasion fleet. The darkness gave way to a curtain of brilliant light; every ship could be seen clearly. The bombs dropped far away behind Portsmouth. I climbed back into my hammock when the all clear sounded and fell asleep.

Eisenhower's message to the invaders was brief:

Soldiers, sailors and airmen of the Allied Expeditionary Force. You are about to embark upon the great crusade, toward which we have striven these many months. The eyes of the world are upon you. The hopes and prayers of liberty-loving people everywhere march with you.

The Isle of Wight was an advanced base for Normandy-bound troops and a major casualty clearing station for those wounded in the invasion. M.E. Littleboy, an ambulance driver with the First Aid Nursing Yeomanry, kept a diary of her nineteen days there:

We [had] had a security lecture over briefed personnel [BPs] who we were likely to have in and who, in their ravings, might blurt out the date and strategy etc. They would be well-labelled 'BP' though and anything we heard we were to forget. We did have a good few cases in though. I believe only one person on the island knew the exact date.

[Monday, 5 June] was a dull and windy day, not June weather at all, and we were cold. But sure enough when we awoke and looked out of our windows, ships [were going past] ... all that day they went by, with never a stop and not more than 100 yards between each vessel. Our excitement and agitation grew as the day went by. We knew this was no exercise. In the evening we were on top of the cliffs, a grandstand view, and our hearts were with these men.

... I slept fitfully and dreamed the whole night of only one thing, the invasion, and I knew before my radio announced it [that] we had our feet in France.

That day we spent with our eyes more or less glued to the sea and never did the boats stop. Stream after stream of them bobbing up and down in the choppy sea and indeed we were sorry for the men on board.

> That day too, the order came out for no more organised parties and a curfew to be in at 11 o'clock and everybody had to be armed. It was a grim sight to see all the officers with their revolvers, some of them two, one on each side, the men with their machine guns, and notices in the flics [cinema] asking them to make sure they were unloaded before sitting down; we all felt very helpless.

The invasion had begun with an airborne assault of more than 24,000 paratroopers from British, American, Canadian and Free French forces. An amphibious attack of over 5,000 ships was to carry more than 160,000 troops to five beaches along a 50-mile stretch of coastline in Normandy. Despite these huge numbers, a rapid German response would be catastrophic.

Wren Shirley Gadsby was listening to the enemy on the French coast:

> The night before was quiet. So quiet that I had the eerie experience of taking down a message from a German aircraft, asking permission from base to return home, as it was obvious to them that nothing was moving! I took very great pleasure in passing this on to the Duty Commander and to Peter Scott, who was with us that night, together with his IC [commanding officer] Christopher Dyer. They had committed their forces and had nothing to do except worry, and asked if they might come and hold hands with us! They would pop out to the plotting room every so often to see the model fleet progressing across the Channel and came back at midnight to say that '*Warspite* has opened fire!' – this being the first shot fired during the operation. Need I say that we had had no messages from our friends the lights and guns … neither did we

have a peep out of anyone that night. Surprise had been total. We had quite a lot to do thereafter.

Dieter Hartmann-Schultze, a panzerjäger (anti-tank) gunner with the 711th Infantry Division, was stationed across the Channel on the Normandy coast. On 5 June, as he was returning with others to his post – in an area which the Allies had marked as a landing point for the British Second Army – military policemen warned him of possible enemy parachutists ahead:

> We were frightened, but decided we must return to our unit as quickly as possible. We saw searchlights and flak and flashes in the sky and once stopped to listen. All we heard was the sound of aircraft, but then it seemed small-arms fire. We consulted our map, trying to decide which route to take. We had no idea where the enemy parachutists could be, if in fact any had landed at all. So we drove on cautiously for another hour until quite suddenly we ran into a German patrol and were made to identify ourselves. The Lieutenant warned us we might run into a paratroop ambush, so we felt even more scared. But we drove on and encountered several more alarms before safely reaching our own unit just before dawn. As soon as we had rested we were told enemy airborne troops were in the area and we must go to our guns. We then heard the sporadic small-arms fire to the east and knew the reports were true – unless it was all an enemy trick and our people were firing at each other!

His first direct encounter with the invasion came soon after. Allied navy ships were to provide a preliminary bombardment and supporting fire for their forces landing on the beaches.

… I ran to join my comrades who were already in a small bunker near our anti-tank battery overlooking the beach. Our guns were 75s and very powerful. Then one of our lookouts raised the alarm in great excitement as he saw the first ships on the horizon through his night binoculars. We rushed outside. It was now lighter and we saw the fantastic fleet which amazed us. And soon we saw the first flashes from the battleships' guns and rushed for cover as the huge shells came rushing over. In shelter we stayed for a whole hour as the terrific cannonade continued, until at last our Sergeant told us to get to our guns. We found to our amazement that only one gun had been damaged, even though a huge number of shells and bombs from planes had fallen about us. There was smoke and the smell of explosives everywhere and as we reached our gun the first smaller calibre fire from weapons on the ships and landing craft began reaching us, so we lay flat and waited.

Wren Rosemary Geddes was listening to the enemy reaction to the sight of the invasion force:

From the south coast we were covering the traffic, mostly W/T [wireless transmissions], between the German gun emplacements across the Channel. The gun crews were practising daily what their procedure should be in the event of an invasion, and there was one operator who always got it wrong and was in constant trouble. When D-Day actually came and there was furious activity from all the gunsites, our unfortunate 'friend' came on the air with a plaintive plea in plain language asking what had happened to his cigarette ration, blissfully unaware that

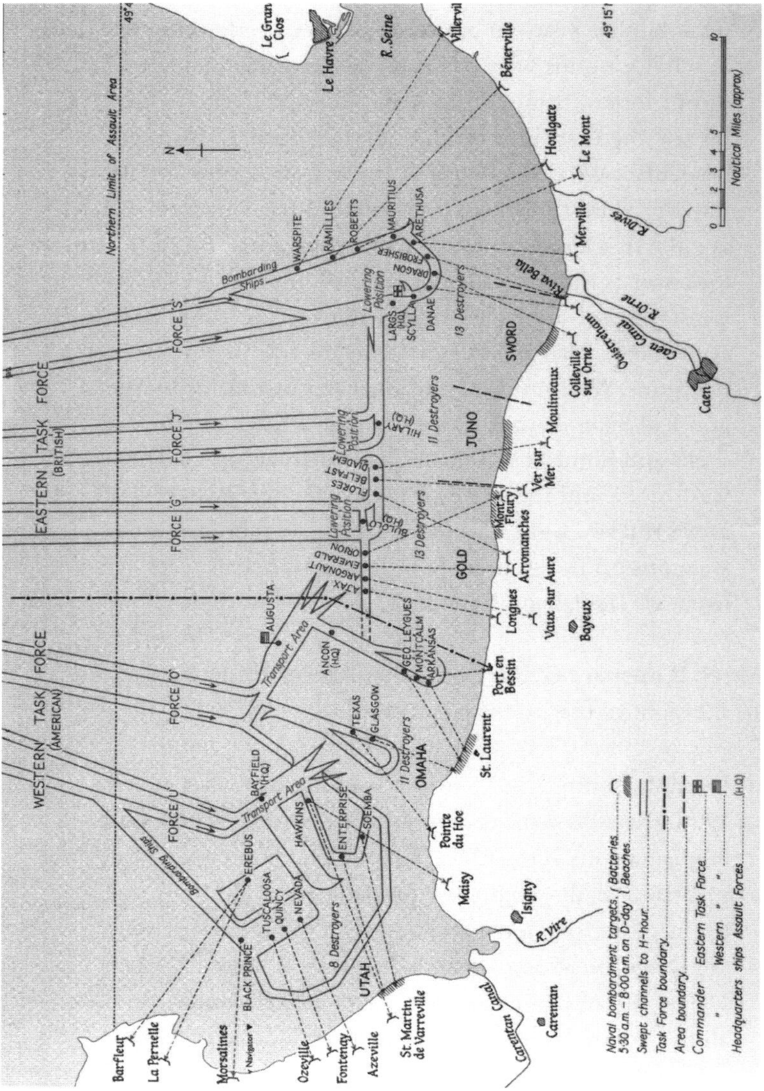

Normandy landings (Crown Copyright)

this time the invasion was for real. I think the rest of the crews nearly turned their guns on him!

But the Allied bombs silenced many of them anyway, and although it was vital to save the lives of our own forces, each call-sign had developed a personality and one was aware of the sad madness of war as one by one the messages ceased.

Commandos were among the first to land in France; they were to attack and take enemy positions which would otherwise take a heavy toll on the incoming forces.

Kenneth Oakley was a leading seaman with Fox Royal Navy Commando:

We boarded our assault ship *Empire Broadsword*. Everyone was fired up for the 'big one' when we were told about the delay because of bad weather.

However the next day found us underway and on the evening of 5th June '44 the senior officer on board had us all assembled, for a chat. He ended with the resounding words: 'Do not worry if you do not survive the assault, as we have plenty of back up troops who will just go in over you.'

It was early, approx. 03.30, and the Beach Master, Lt. John Bruick, RNVR and I boarded the LCA to run for our target … which was about five miles away. The sea was rough and several of the soldiers on board were sea sick, but as we ploughed along I could see that all around us were landing craft and warships of all shapes and sizes.

As I sighted the plough formation of stars ahead of us, the roar of the naval bombardment passed overhead and soon we heard the chatter of small arms fire directed at us.

The LCA flotilla taking us to our target area was doing a great job by keeping us almost exactly on course.

Off to our port side an LCT discharged a salvo of rockets in the direction of the Merville battery we had been briefed about. We evaded all the small arms fire, but suddenly the dreaded steel stakes with mines or shells attached, loomed ahead of us.

Daylight was with us now, and the cox of our LCA did very well to miss a shell attached to a stake on our starboard side, and then we heard the order 'Down Ramps' and our time had come.

It was 06.10am … and the Beach Master and I were quickly out of the craft and running up the sandy beach as mortar and machine-gun fire sped us on our way. At the high water mark we went to ground to take stock of the situation and get our bearings. John said we had landed almost exactly in our scheduled area, but as the mortar fire became more intense we wriggled deeper in the sand. My task was to protect and help the BM at all times, but when a stricken paratrooper cried out for help, it was difficult to stay with the BM and ignore the cries.

Lieutenant Harry Jones was leader of 10 Platoon, 'X' Company, the King's Shropshire Light Infantry. He later recalled that on 5 June:

We re-embarked on the landing craft, carefully cleaned and oiled our weapons, double-checked our equipment and tried to catch up with some much-needed sleep. Later that evening we slipped out of Newhaven harbour heading south-west. We still had no idea of our destination except that we had ascertained from previous briefings that it was somewhere on the northern coast of France.

The night crossing was choppy, but I did manage to get a couple of hours sleep. I rolled out of my bunk the following morning at about six o clock, tried to stand up on the rolling deck, washed and shaved and swallowed a couple of anti-seasickness pills which, together with a 'bags, vomit one', had thoughtfully been issued to us! When I went up on deck it was daylight and I could hardly believe my eyes – the Channel was filled with ships of all descriptions – battleships, cruisers, destroyers, minesweepers and hundreds of all types of landing craft, many of them flying barrage balloons. Overhead were hundreds of aircraft all heading for the French coast – American Flying Fortress bombers, Lightning and Mustang fighters, RAF Lancaster bombers, Spitfire, Hurricane and Typhoon fighters. It was a sight I shall never forget. I remembered reading Shakespeare's Henry V in school:

> And gentlemen in England now a-bed,
> Will think themselves accurs'd they were not here.

Below deck again, I opened a sealed envelope and took out the map of the coastal area in northern France upon which we were to land. It was in Normandy, and the beach we were to assault was code-named Sword, the most easterly of all the landing beaches, and therefore closest to the main German Tank Divisions. Our sector of Sword beach was Queen beach, with the French town of Hermanville a mile or two inland. 3rd British Infantry Division's objectives ran from the coast to Caen.

Austin Baker remembered:

We eventually sailed off down the Solent at midday on June 5th. Major Barker called all the 4th/7th chaps into the captain's cabin, which was about the size of a double bed, and told us where we were headed. It turned out to be a little place between Caen and Arromanches called La Rivière. Our particular stretch of the beach was known as King Red beach, and our rendezvous was at the village of Ver-sur-mer.

Major B. read out messages from Eisenhower and Montgomery and told us that he personally thought we should all be very honoured to be in on this affair. I think most of us felt that we could have stood the disgrace of being left out of it.

The fleet hove to for a time, to get organised, and it was midnight before we sailed past the Needles. It was very rough and the LCT bounced around a good deal. Most of the people on board were sick but I was lucky, as I've never been sea-sick in my life.

We bedded down, but I don't suppose any of us slept very much.

The naval and air bombardment was scheduled to start at 6.25, and we were all up and ready long before that. As it grew light we could see LCTs stretching in line astern as far as the eye could see, and another line steamed on a parallel course a mile or two away. Overhead a big formation of American bombers – Mitchells or Marauders I think – were heading in to start the bombardment.

The first sight of the French coast gave me a queer feeling. Everybody stared at it without saying very much as we slowly drew towards it, passing the big troopships which lay at anchor, having sent their infantry on towards the beach in small assault boats.

There were several cruisers lying out there too, firing broadside after broadside inland. We passed within a couple of hundred yards of one, which I seem to remember was the *Belfast* – the noise of her guns was ear-splitting. There was a battleship firing in the distance – the *Rodney*, so the skipper announced over the loud hailer on the bridge.

Two squadrons of rocket-firing Typhoons [aircraft] roared over – after the 88 [German cannon] which we knew was on the beach according to Lieut. Ford, the IO (intelligence officer).

If they were, they didn't get it. The 88 knocked out two Churchills before we arrived and was itself knocked out by a 'flail' tank. We saw a terrific explosion onshore, which was presumably one of the Churchills going up.

There were destroyers right in close to the beach, firing like mad. They must have been almost aground. Rocket ships – LCTs carrying batteries of rocket guns – and SP [self-propelled] guns firing from LCTs added to the general din.

Smoke hung over everything and we could see the flashes of exploding shells on land. We couldn't tell which way they were arriving.

About half a mile from the beach a navy motor-boat drifted past with a dead sailor lying across the foredeck. I'd never seen anybody dead before.

We were still two or three hundred yards offshore when a big spout of water shot up near our starboard side, followed by another in almost the same place. 'We are now being shelled', the skipper said dramatically. It was very naval and unpleasant.

By now the beach was black with men and machines, and scores of LCTs were discharging their cargoes. The sea was still rough and obviously making things very difficult. I saw several lorries overturn in the breakers.

Our LCT went in and the bows touched bottom. Handling it must have been tricky, as the beach was lined with metal spikes, some with Teller mines fixed to them. Before the ramp could be lowered the current swung the craft round and the skipper had to back her out again among the infantry who were wading ashore up to their necks in water.

We went in a second time and weren't so lucky. There was a terrific crash and the LCT jerked back. It had hit one of the mines. I was sitting in my seat at the time, with my head sticking out of the hatch – the operator seat on an ARV being next to the driver's. I was thrown forward and hit my mouth on the rim of the hatch, breaking a tooth and making me feel a bit dizzy. I lowered the seat quickly, shut the hatch and watched things through the periscope. The Number One, who had been standing in the bows, had been blown into the air. I think he broke a couple of ribs, but he got up and carried on directing the lowering of the ramp, which was damaged but went down OK.

Captain Collins's scout car was first down the ramp and it was immediately knocked out by a shell. Collins was unhurt but Steeles, his driver, was wounded. All the rest of the vehicles got safely ashore.

Sergeant Thomas Kilvert was with 77 Assault Squadron, in command of AVRE 1C:

We stood at dawn on board the LCT 100A at 0500 hours. Breakfast was on, but nobody really wanted it, being more or less seasick. I had the AVRE 1C started up, all guns loaded and a last minute check over the tank. It was now about 0610 hours and the coastline stood out in the haze; we were coming in fast.

About half a mile out everyone mounted their tanks. Almost in, 400 yards to go when 1C had a violent shake: we had been hit. Damage not known because the LCT had also sustained damage a bit forward and we had to get off at once.

The LCT stopped: H. Howe and H. George in front moved off; again 1C was hit. Going up the ramp now and the water was almost up to our cupola. Again we were hit but on our bobbin, it being at a crazy angle. Coming up out of the water, hit again, and at last dry, and following 1A up the sand. Hit a mine, one bogie gone, but following on in 1A's track, we were ordered to put up a windsock, 1A having lost his. Struck a second mine, two bogies and left track gone.

L/Cpl Fairlie and Sapper Vaughan jumped out to put up a windsock. L/Cpl Fairlie was blown up by a mine as he came round the tank. I ordered abandon tank, take all arms, and jumped out myself, destroyed 'Slidex and code papers'. We were all out now, petrol was pouring out of 1C and filling the mine crater.

Everyone lay down whilst I looked for the L/Cpl's remains. None found so I returned and organised the crew into a fighting patrol. Just then L/Sgt Freer from 3 troop joined us; he had swum ashore from his tank which had been on our LCT.

Back in England, the *Assiduous* was preparing to leave. T. Osbourne recalled:

> [I] … woke to hear the throbbing sound of diesel engines; hundreds of landing and escort ships were moving toward the open sea. Overhead, aircraft of every type were moving in unending streams toward France. All had white stripes on their wings [so they would recognise each other as Allied aircraft].
>
> We also started moving and joined the great stream of ships. Joining us were other rescue tugs in a convoy of two-column formation. Our escorts were motor torpedo boats that were very patient with us. We realised many of the smaller landing craft were having difficulty steering straight courses and some had stopped altogether, presumably with engine trouble. *Assiduous* kept its position in the convoy as the coast of England receded in the distance.
>
> … The sound of guns and bombs could be heard in the distance and soon I could see the flashes from the warship guns. The ship was now close enough to the shore to see and hear the screaming sigh of the rockets leaving the LCRs. Great clouds of smoke enveloped the coastline as dusk settled around us. Now there was a real danger of collision as the Dan buoys that lit up the mine-swept areas were small. A large landing craft near us blew up; obviously one of the mines had been missed. I thought of the soldiers and her crew who were surely dead as the vessel was a mass of flames and explosions from end-to-end.
>
> We passed another floating mine on our port bow, and not 15 minutes later another on our starboard bow. The whole ship's company was nervous. An officer, normally

the gentlest of men, shouted at me; I was exhausted. I went below to sleep, and awakened by a smack on the face, tipped out of my hammock, and told that we were under attack. I ran back to the boat deck and two of the older members of the crew made a place for me near the shelter of our gun pit. They put their arms around me; I realised that I was trembling.

Now it was a question of my mind's endurance and the return of my conscious self. The desperate truth is a child cannot find comfort from frightened adults and I was still a child. It was impossible to tell which vessels were engaged in the fighting; every few minutes arcs of red tracers criss-crossed the sky. Thus far, we had not fired and I was thankful, being acutely aware we were sitting ducks. Orange, red and white flares suddenly burst into the night sky. Later the roar of the engines came and fast black shapes raced across the flare-lit sea. Rapid cannon and machine gun fire could be heard. There was a huge flaming explosion ahead of us followed by another on our starboard bow; our own twin 20mm guns opened fire at the racing shapes; tracer shell fire curved through the air from every ship. The deep rumble of the heavy guns continued to be heard and the horizon was lit up to the south. It was a sure sign that a great battle was being waged for possession of the beach.

C. Fenwick served in the RAF Air Sea Rescue Service. He was stationed at Dover, rescuing survivors from damaged ships in the invasion armada. Writing in 1949, he recalled that, at 2.00 p.m. on 6 June, the Germans began firing their massive cross-Channel guns at the invasion fleet:

Having no protecting smoke screen, the convoy was a sitting target. A Liberty boat was soon straddled with shells.

We were soon ordered back to sea to pick up survivors. What a sight I witnessed as we, at maximum speed, roared out towards a scene I will always remember. A large blazing mess of a once-proud ship, fires, fore and aft, some lifeboats suspended crazily over the side, soldiers and merchant seamen diving off in frantic haste. The ammunition in its cargo of lorries cracking off as the spreading fires reached them. There was a constant danger of it blowing up at any time! As far as I could see, the sea was dotted with men, a few lifeboats upturned, and one, so full with survivors that they were slowly sinking it.

Fortune favoured them all in one respect. The sea was relatively calm off Dover, just a slight lazy swell from the storm yesterday.

On the seaward side of the ships, a lone motor launch was having some trouble in effecting a smoke screen to protect us all. Many wounded men unable to help themselves much were being swept swiftly away by the strong current which runs in this part of the Channel. I observed one helpless man and reported this to our captain. Our eyes met for a split second and he made his decision: 'I am a stronger swimmer than you, I will go.' There was not a moment to lose as the gap was widening between our stationary launch and the soldier. The skipper dived overboard. A capable swimmer he made good headway with strong clean strokes. He reached him and turned towards us with his man. The launch, all engines stopped, was drifting away from the skipper and the danger was obvious. I drew the coxswain's attention to this and he started up one engine and we moved towards the swimmer and his burden – a slow operation otherwise the soldiers in the water around us would be run down in the process. Eventually the skipper was hauled alongside with his man and they were hauled aboard. A very gallant effort living fully up to the ASRS slogan 'the sea shall not have them'.

The work of rescue continued. There were two soldiers in the water a few yards away. One was silent and the other, a massive fellow, [who] was wildly thrashing the water and whose cries for help had alerted me in that direction. The quiet one heaved himself up the rope crash ladder. To my astonishment, I noticed he was hopping up on only one leg! The other had been blown off and the stump was just a piece of jagged flesh. Our young MO made him comfortable.

I turned my attention to the other one gazing upwards towards me, who was in danger of drowning through sheer panic. I decided the only way was to go over the side of the boat and so encourage him that way. I entreated him to grasp the bottom of the crash ladder, I placed my shoulder under him in an attempt to help him up. It was too much as he was at least 14 stone, he failed to hold on to the ladder and the great bulk of his sea-drenched body crashed down on me in the water. I went under and I knew no more.

Fortunately the rest of the boat crew were close and managed to save us both.

Soon afterwards, our launch, loaded to capacity with survivors, turned towards Dover. The massive guns from France were still blazing away and falling between the convoy and the rescue ships. The stricken Liberty ship, still on fire, drifted towards the high promontory of Shakespeare cliff.

Wren Veronica Owen was in the communications centre in Southwick, a mansion near the village in Hampshire, which was the headquarters for D-Day planning. In a letter to her parents, written on the night of 5/6 June, she hoped that, now the invasion had started, the war would soon be over:

> … it is now Tuesday evening and what a day. I still can't believe we have actually landed in France that which we've all been waiting and waiting for such ages should at last have happened and so far apparently so successfully. Captain Sinker told each office individually last evening about 9.00 that 'we were off'. You can imagine even though we could split the watch there wasn't much sleep for anyone! The security seems to have been magnificent and I believe it really must have been a bit of a surprise – gosh I wouldn't have been anywhere else today nor nowhere else last night – we were lucky to have been on watch for the beginning. The fall of Rome is a marvellous bit of news isn't it and I suppose soon the Russians will start cracking and the Germans will soon find themselves so hemmed in it will be impossible for them to dig themselves out.

The continuing bad weather both helped and hindered the invaders: it prevented air attacks on the German defences on, in particular, Omaha and Juno beaches from being effective but at the same time it reinforced the German military view that the Normandy landings were a diversionary tactic – the Allies would not attempt a full-scale landing in such conditions.

The Allied naval bombardment was a success not only in providing supporting fire for the landing forces but also in preventing the enemy from forming up effectively as they tried to regroup inland.

5

On the Beaches: Sword and Juno

The Atlantic Wall – the German defences along the French coastline – was believed by many to be impregnable, among them Field Marshal von Rundstedt, who was in charge of the defence of Western Europe. However, General Rommel, von Rundstedt's subordinate and the enemy leader most respected by the Allies, was more sceptical. In the first half of 1944, Hitler sent Rommel to inspect the Atlantic Wall and make recommendations. As a result, Rommel ordered tons of steel and concrete to be brought in to reinforce the defences; the beaches were littered with tank traps and mines, and possible landing places were overlooked by machine-gun nests.

Despite their encouraging and stirring speeches, Eisenhower and his commanders feared that the largest invasion force in history would be stopped even from landing by heavy German opposition. Eisenhower carried with him a message for the troops to be broadcast in the event of failure.

However, the numerous Allied deception operations had been effective. German forces were convinced that any Allied invasion would be made through the Pas-de-Calais; so much so that even after the invasion had begun, they believed the Normandy landings to be a diversion. As a result, German reserves of tanks and troops were held back at Calais, ready for the supposed real assault, until it was too late to bring them into battle against the invaders. Communications were widely disrupted and reports of landings could not be co-ordinated.

Crucially, too, on the night of the 5/6 June, the bad weather in northern France also persuaded German commanders that an imminent invasion was impossible. So, as the invasion began, General Rommel and other senior officers were absent; many were on a training exercise, while Rommel was with his family, celebrating his wife's birthday.

The invasion forces were to land on five beaches: the British forces' and the Free French commandos' target beaches were codenamed Sword and Gold; those on which American forces were to land were called Utah and Omaha, and combined Canadian and British forces were to land on Juno. The easternmost beach was Sword, then, moving westwards, Juno, Gold, Omaha and Utah.

Sword

Sword Beach, was a flat, sandy, 5-mile stretch of coastline dotted with small villages. It was divided into four sectors: Oboe, Peter, Queen and Roger.

The plan was that the first Allied troops to land would be the British 3rd Infantry Division, led by 8th Infantry Brigade Group. Once they had fought their way off the beach through Queen sector, they were to move inland towards the city of Caen, where they were to link up with airborne troops who were protecting the eastern flank.

From midnight on 6 June, the airborne troops, arriving in gliders and planes, seized the eastern flanks, including the bridge at Bénouville, and the long-range guns in the

German battery at Merville. The beach landings were then preceded by a huge bombardment of the German positions by warships and aircraft, before troops began to arrive on Sword just before 7.30 a.m.

DD (duplex drive – specialist 'swimming') tanks and 'funnies' (General Hobart's specialised tanks) landed with teams of Royal Engineers, to knock out numerous enemy gun positions. Royal Engineers, whose task was to clear the way of obstacles, were first on the beaches. However, rough seas and fierce currents severely hampered the landings from the start and held up the tanks.

Major Maximilian de L'Orme was an officer with the Royal Engineers, commanding 263 Field Company on Sword:

> When dawn broke, we were lying close to a large destroyer which, 'out of the blue', seemed to fold up and sink, all in a few minutes – which was a little unnerving. Not a single one of us had even a tinge of sea-sickness until that time.

The destroyer he refers to is the *Svenner*, a ship of the Norwegian navy, which was struck by two torpedoes at dawn on 6 June. Out of its crew of 219, thirty-three were killed and 185 rescued, of whom fifteen were wounded. *Svenner* was the only Allied ship to be sunk by German naval activity on D-Day.

Major de L'Orme recorded how the weather and the resulting high seas hampered the invaders:

> ... the sea had really 'got up' and the small landing craft were dodging about like corks. We all trooped on to the larger craft – even that was quite a feat, especially as each

man had in addition to his assault kit, two small boxes of explosives, and ten made up fuses. I had to brief the two captains of the craft as to where we were going, and we eventually set off as a little convoy …

The skipper of the LCI's said he would land us 'dry shod'; quite sure about it he was. The choppiness had altered the seasickness state, and at least 25 per cent were quite bad before we had been on board ten minutes.

As we came within 800 yards of the shore, we came under shellfire from shore batteries, and both were hit several times; one of my men and several others were killed, and some of the sailors injured. As we came closer, the skipper saw the difficulty of getting us ashore and being able to clear again, for there were several disabled carriers and other wrecks about, and he said he would have to stand off in 'wading depth'. His idea of wading was a little sketchy, and we stepped off the walk-ways into about 5ft 6 inches of lovely cold water – still all complete with boxes of explosives etc. The non-swimmers – luckily very few – were literally dragged along the bottom, but we lost no men from drowning in landing craft. Other landing craft were not so lucky, only five of them were able to touch down and disembark their load – the others were swept away from the beach and all were subjected to intense gunfire … Another carrier struck a mine immediately on touching down and was blown up, and another overturned in the water. Eventually four carriers were salvaged, but even they had lost a lot of their stores by action of the sea. Altogether the disembarkation of the carriers was rather a failure – this being in no way the fault of the crews but entirely due to the heavy seas and enemy fire. The majority of the explosive and initiators, and about 13 Polish mine detectors were salvaged by our men and stacked at the top of the beach.

H.T. Bone was a lieutenant in the 2nd Battalion, East Yorkshire Regiment. In a letter to his mother, dated July 1944, he wrote of his work in charge of a signals unit on Sword beach on D-Day:

> As our flotilla swung into line behind its leader we raised our flag, a black silk square with the White Rose of Yorkshire in the centre. The Navy had sewn their red anchor into the top left-hand corner and the Brass Marine badge was soldered to the blade of the spear on which the flag was suspended dead. It blew taut in the wind and spray. As we left the ship our bugler blew the General Salute and then again as we passed the HQ ship, the Senior Officer returning our CO's salute. It was some distance to the beaches and it was a wet trip. All of us had a spare gas cape to keep us dry and chewed our gum stolidly. Mine was still in my mouth 12 or 14 hours later, and usually I hate the stuff and never touch it. Shielding ourselves from the spray and watching the fire going down from all the supporting arms and the spits overhead the time soon passed. Promptly at H hour I began listening on the wireless sets for the first news. It was a very dull morning and the land was obscured by mist and smoke, so that except for the flotilla leader and the CO, no one actually saw the land till the metal doors opened in front and the ramp was down, but very soon after H hour, crystal clear over my set came messages from the assaulting companies. By now we could hear the tach-a-tach-a-tach of enemy machine guns and the strident explosions of

German prisoners wait beside a disabled Sherman 'Crab' flail tank. (Sgt J. Mapham, No.5 Army Film & Photographic Unit. Crown Copyright)

enemy mortars on the beach and its approaches. Now was the moment – we clutched our weapons and wireless sets, all carefully waterproofed. A shallow beach, we had been told, wet up to our knees or a little over, and then a long stretch of sand and obstacles. Suddenly there was a jarring bump on the left and looking up from our boards we saw some of the beach obstacles about two feet above our large gunwale with a large mine on top of it, just as photographs had shown us; the mine just the same as those we had practised disarming. Again a bump on the right, but still we had not grounded. The colonel and the flotilla leader were piloting us in, and for a few brief minutes nothing happened except the music of the guns and the whang of occasional bullets overhead, with the sporadic explosions of mortar bombs and the background of our own heavy fire. Then the doors opened as we grounded and the colonel was out. The sea was choppy and the boat swung a good bit as one by one we followed him. Several fell in and got soaked through. I was lucky. I stopped for a few seconds to help my men with their heavy wireless sets and to ensure they kept them dry. As we staggered ashore we dispersed and lay down above the water's edge. Stuff was falling pretty close to us and although I did not see it happen, quite a number of people from my own boat were hit. Instinctively where we lay we hacked holes with our shovels. The colonel moved forward. I tried to collect my party of sets and operators, but could only see a few of them. I began to recognise wounded men of the assault companies. Some were dead, others struggling to crawl out of the water because the tide was rising very rapidly. We could not help since our job was to push on, but I saw one of my signal corporals with a wound in his leg and I took his codes with me, promising to send a man back for his set before he was evacuated. Getting just off the beach among some ruined buildings we began to collect the HQ. The other boat party was mostly missing, also three quarters of my sets. The colonel was getting a grip on the battle and I was sent back on the beach to collect the rest of us. I did not feel afraid, but rather elated and full of beans. There were some horrible sights there and not a few men calling out for help. I had no time or duty there, the beach medical people would gradually get round to them all. Under the sides of a tank that had been hit I saw a bunch of my people and I bawled out at them to get up and get moving since they were doing no good there and could quite safely get along to HQ. I felt a little callous when I found that nearly all of them had been hit and some were dead. But sorting them out I made up half the wireless team and then went in search of some more.

Further on were the adjutant and the padre with their party, also taking cover. I told them where we were and took them back with me. By persuading a couple of blokes with shrapnel in their legs and feet that they were good for a few hours yet, I got my wireless lifted and we got back to HQ. It was just moving off further inland. Later I discovered that Jimmy Laurie and Major Barber, one of my signallers and numerous others, had been killed on the beach landing at the same time as myself, and I felt I had been very fortunate.

The next battle I saw only from the back, but its aftermath gave me my first real taste of fear. We had moved forward into one already taken enemy position to mount an attack on a stronger one beyond it. This was rash since Jerry had his mortars laid on the last position. It was a small thick wood by the side of a road, and he fairly laced into us. I cannot tell you how many were wounded and killed there, but I lost some more signallers and a whole crowd round me got hit. We could not get away, neither could we dig. The ground was hard and tangled with roots, the bombs were bursting literally everywhere all the time. I laid on my face for a few moments, then seeing the provost sergeant hit five yards away I pushed over to him and shoved my field dressing on the back of his neck. He had a piece through his shoulder, but it was not serious, and we got him out of it. (Curious how everyone turns yellow when hit.)

We all had to get out of it and we did. The attack went in from the rear instead and was successful, lots of Jerry prisoners being captured, but Dicky was killed and Hurch wounded, as well as a good many others. After this, having reached our objectives, all but one, we began to collect ourselves. People get lost all over the place in battle, some deliberately, most quite by accident. We were pulled back a bit and made to dig in for the night, but we got very little sleep, and next day moved on and dug in again and so on – the rest since then I cannot yet tell you, but D-Day was not the end, nor is the end yet. Thank God Clive, Tony and Ronnie and Bill are still alive and well. For the rest, it is a tale of new faces. PS Don't let this story depress you because we are in great form now.

Captain A. Low commanded 2 Troop, 77 Assault Squadron, which came under heavy fire:

At this time the Navy was bringing down heavy fire on the beaches and the RAF were bombing it to hell …

It was vital that the adapted tanks – Hobart's Funnies – made it on to the beach first ... All craft were ordered to stop the engines to allow them through. ...

LCTs were then ordered to beach at full speed ... The craft were attacked by four planes with British markings, two bombs landing very close to our doorway. Two Oerlikon guns on the craft were being used both against the aircraft and the houses on the beach, which contained snipers and machine guns, whose sole purpose in life was to make the bridge of the craft uninhabitable. I scrambled down to my tank, ordering L/Cpl Parsons and Sapper Manuel to cut holding ropes on fascine bundles on the port side of the craft.

Ahead of us was a gun which was apparently concentrating on the troop on our left. Sgt Smyth ran his flail up to high water mark and begun flailing straight for the gun. Cpl Nash followed, widening the gap.

Major Ferguson ran his AVRE off the craft and began an attempt to clear obstacles on the beach. I followed out with the Boase carpet, running up to the gun and turning right along the flail path.

Sgt Smyth had flailed a second path up to the sand dunes, and this I used to push the Boase Bangalore into a sand dune about six feet high. During this time, Sgt Myhill was running up the beach with his bridge. He dropped it on the edge of the gun position but apparently experienced trouble in releasing the bottom end. He leapt out of the turret and dealt with it.

I was experiencing trouble in cutting the rope tackle on the Bangalore, which had been pushed very easily into the dunes, as snipers kept up a steady hail of lead whenever I appeared ...

By this time grenades were being thrown at my tank, so I poked my head out and dealt with the offender, then cutting the Bangalore loose. During the drive back from the dune I saw the Bangalore explode, having been hit. It made a good gap in the dunes, but I did not drop the carpet on it as both flails had gone forward.

The beach was being shelled, and snipers were very active. Running back along to the bridge we started to mount it, but the right support of the carpet was blown away and the logs dropped on to the bridge. We drew back and stopped, Spr Young, L/Cpl Parsons, Spr Manuel and I got out and attached a tow rope to the last log, and the AVRE pulled the carpet back off the bridge. Some Pioneers were lying behind and at the side of the tank under cover. These I ordered to help straighten out the carpet to form a straight run on to the bridge. We eventually did the job, but for four logs, on our own.

We nipped back into the tank and crossed the bridge … The infantry who had landed right behind us were now pushing forward. As we reached the top of the bridge, I saw Cpl Nash standing behind his flail which had struck a mine, breaking a track.

Sgt Myhill reported that he had cleared the roadway 300 yards along to the right. I ordered him to turn around and contact 1 Tp on the left, but I reached 1 Tp myself before he did.

A call from Maj Ferguson informed me that the windsock was not flying, and Sgt Myhill went back to the beach to chase it up. He did not reappear so I went along to the beach on foot, being unable to clear my tanks on the crossroads although the second lateral was being shelled and mortared.

On reaching the beach, I discovered that only a part-coloured windsock had been available and the yellow had been torn off to make a fully coloured one. This windsock had been erected by Sgt Myhill, Cpl Arnold and Spr Spiers. Having completed the erection of the sock, the men were getting back in the AVRE when a machine gun opened up, killing Sgt Myhill and wounding Spr Spiers.

Major de L'Orme was one of many in the wrong place:

The scene on the beach was indescribable – an absolute inferno, burning tanks, broken down vehicles, and very many dead and wounded lying about in a narrow strip between the sea and the wire at the back of the beach. There were shells, mortars and the occasional bomb falling, and a considerable amount of small arms fire. For a few moments I thought none of the things we had planned had come to pass. We were nearly one and a half hours late, the tide was almost high, we were all on Red beach near La Brêche, instead of spread along the whole of Queen. Our task of clearing beach obstacles was obviously hopeless, so I organised four sections into parties for clearing beach exits and laying track to try and clear some of the congestion. We spread over half the beach and soon had about six exits commenced, and had contacted some of the mechanical equipment.

Major William Carruthers MC, leader of 3 Troop, 77 Assault Squadron, encountered German troops almost immediately:

We moved into the beach, the ramp door was down in no time, and the two flails followed by an AVRE were rumbling up the beach. I had the task of guiding them into the gap as they were both blind due to flailing. Once they were in line I had a chance to look around, and the bridge layer, bobbin AVRE and armoured bulldozer were successfully ashore. The bobbin AVRE had stopped in the water and the crew were baling out (later it was found they had blown a track on a Tellermine), but the bridge layer and bulldozer were alright.

At that moment three very frightened Germans came running down the beach 'Hande Hoch', were waved on, and to our amazement and amusement ran into the sea still 'Hande Hoch'.

Major Carruthers was attempting to clear and establish gaps in the defences through which the incoming troops and equipment could go up the beach and inland:

As I was to follow the flails through the gap, I asked my gunner to lay the log carpet in the gap, but this and the turret had jammed and I had to cut it loose – the log carpet, unfortunately, as a result fell in a heap and formed more of an obstacle than a road. While I was doing this, there was a bang, flash, red lights, blue lights etc, and I found myself lying on the sand, having been hit by a hand grenade thrown from the house alongside the tank. I was assured later by a flail commander that the thrower had a 90mm shell all to himself in return.

As I could now not hold the microphone, I ordered the troop sergeant to cover the flails in my tank – while I carried on gapping, checking and marking with the remainder of the troop. The bulldozer got to work and in 15 to 20 minutes the first gap was good enough for both tracks and wheels.

Troops on Sword Beach wait for the signal to advance. (Sgt J. Mapham, No.5 Army Film & Photographic Unit. Crown Copyright)

At this time it is as well to describe the beach. In the planning we had expected a 400 yards stretch of beach; on arrival we found it to be 100 yards. As a result, most of the obstacles were in the water with only their tops showing, making the task for the beach clearing teams, composed of AVREs and 629 [Field Squadron], extremely difficult. Quite a large number of SP guns, Bofors, carriers, infantry etc, had concentrated on landing, and beach parties were trying to dig in everywhere to avoid the mortar fire and sniping that was quite unhealthy. The movement control for the moment seemed temporarily suspended.

Near the gap a few minutes after the hand grenade episode, it was reported to me that Lt Dickinson was wounded. I found him lying by an AVRE looking very sick with a nasty hole in his shoulder. It appeared that he had gone out on a Sherman removing Tellermines from the obstacles, when he had been hit. He had to be brought ashore by his hair, held by the Sherman tank commander. However, a mouthful of 'White Horse' [whisky] and a sling worked miracles and he carried on.

We heard immediately on landing that Lt. Colonel A.D. Cocks had been killed, and this was a sad blow to all ranks of the regiment.

Further hitches occurred whilst gapping was in progress and transport being passed through. The first was the armoured bulldozer, which blew a track on a mine. I jumped on it to see if the crew of two were all right. I found them both chuckling with relief at being unhurt. The dozer was pulled clear, and the crew immediately brewed up a tin of self-heating cocoa – I'm sure the first in the assault, a mouthful of which was very welcome.

The two flails reported back to the beach, both commanders having been killed by sniping. One of them, Sgt Andrews of 22 Dragoons, had baled out three times in France in 1940, fought in the Spanish Civil War and had caught it straight away on returning for his revenge. I was extremely sorry to lose him.

The second gap was made using the bridge and running through the gardens between two houses – this was very soon in use with windsocks flying. 185th Infantry Brigade arrived, the follow-through brigade, and cycled off very quickly and efficiently in the direction of Caen.

Owing to the gap control parties not arriving, the movement control on the gaps had to be done by my sappers. Lt Dickinson and myself met Lt Col Urquhart and he told us to report to the beach dressing station. We sent a message to our squadron leader and then reported sick, feeling extremely ill but relieved that things were going well.

Lieutenant Ivan Dickinson, who was Major Carruthers' second-in-command gave his own accounts of clearing obstacles on Sword beach:

Suddenly we saw the first row of obstacles loom out of the smoke. They were ten feet high and consisted of a vertical log capped by a Tellermine, and reinforced on the seaward side by the ramps The door was dropped, the gapping team went ashore and carried on with their job.

While gapping was in progress, the obstacle clearance team disembarked.

Obstacles from a depth of ten feet to 4 feet 6 inches were the responsibility of the Landing Craft Obstacle Clearance Units of the Royal Navy, and those from 4 feet 6 inches to 0 feet were a sapper's responsibility. Each beach, White and Red, was allotted five AVREs for obstacle clearance. Our latest information before leaving was that the obstacles were laid in four rows in the following order from the dunes to the sea:

(a) Two rows of hedgehogs
(b) Stakes
(c) Ramped stakes

The intention was to land with the tide lapping the bottoms of the ramped stakes (c). We were to pass through these, drop our porpoises (waterproofed steel sledges carrying ammunition and explosives) on the beach, and then return, remove such mines as we found on the ramped stakes and then either run them down or tow them away. Having completed row (c) we were to go to (b), and so on. We had prepared two methods of doing this:

By towing – for this a series of slings had been attached to the back of the AVREs, and to those were hooked smaller subsidiary slings by the following personnel, the latter slings having first been attached to the obstacle which it was required to shift.

By blowing – for this we had prepared waterproofed charges which were to be used to blow the obstacles.

These methods had been worked out and practised at Littlehampton prior to the invasion. In addition, immediately on landing we were to erect beacons for the Navy to enable them to navigate into clear areas. We had all this drill firmly set and it was with this in mind that we had set out for Normandy.

The conditions we met were very different. Firstly and most important, the sea was rough and 4 feet up the ramped stakes, secondly there were Tellermines on every stake and shells on all the hedgehogs. This we took in as we came ashore. Soon we had more trouble ...

One of the obstacle clearance [armoured vehicles] ... was an hour late in arriving. As a result, the right hand sector of White beach had had two AVREs and their crews, and the left-hand sector and crew. One of the AVREs received a direct hit, killing two of the crew, and that left two AVREs with twelve men to do something about clearing the obstacles on White beach.

We began by removing shells from the 'hedgehogs' and stacking them in German weapon slits. We then towed the obstacles away. The main problem, however, was the Tellermines on the stakes. We had been given orders to save these mines for future use, so, as soon as a flail had completed its flogging, it was taken into the sea to act as a platform, and we went from stake to stake removing the mines. The waves were breaking over the top of the turret, and so the commander had to keep closed down, while the man on the outside removed the mines. Then we received the unwelcome attention of a machine gunner in one of the beach villas who, after some very poor shooting at 75 yards range, succeeded in scoring an outer. By this time, the waves were too high, so we had to come ashore just before the flail engine gave out. The mines were removed from the back of the tank, and put in disused German defences.

On our sector of the beach we did not put up any navigational beacons for the Navy, as had we done so they would have assumed that the sector of the beach bounded by these was clear, which was not the case.

We then kept the roads off the beach open, and kept traffic moving in whatever way we could.

When the tide began to go down, all the obstacle clearance teams began to clear the beach, and by nightfall had accomplished their task. Meanwhile, the gapping AVREs made their way to their prearranged rendezvous and proceeded to sort themselves out ready for their next tasks.

For the work done on D-Day, 77 and 79 Assault Squadrons between them won two DSOs, four MCs, two DCMs, and three MMs. The Assault Engineers, though hardly any of their number had seen action previously, had proved their worth, and made the Bull's Head a Division sign of which they were all very proud.

Sapper A.J. Lane, was following up close behind the initial assault and could see the gapping and obstacle clearance teams ahead of him taking heavy casualties,

> [with] … shot and shell coming from all frontal directions. I remember my first moments of dragging myself out of the sea holding on to my Bren gun, magazine boxes and other kit. I looked around to see instant death and destruction all around me. But I was conscious that, even so, the beach was perhaps no worse than staying on the boat where I felt I should have died of sea sickness anyways.
>
> I sought cover behind an AVRE which had just been hit. I moved away quickly enough when I realised it was blazing away and that with its petrol, explosive charges etc., it could blow up at any second. I succeeded in making for the bank of dunes at the high tide mark. I hoped that somehow I could get my Bren gun into a position to fire over and beyond the dunes into the enemy direction, wherever that might be.
>
> I remembered as well as anything else that happened then – dammed silly considering the circumstances – my annoyance and irritation at the sea lice or beach bugs, or whatever they were, that were crawling all over me as I itched, above all, to get my Bren gun alive and kicking to some good purpose. An attacking position was not easy because of the mortars, shells and bullets that were hammering down on to a relatively small and concentrated area. There were at least two occasions when I was sure I was an open invitation to shells or mortar

[which were] making direct hits on soldiers moving close to me – the phenomenon of seeing them literally disappear in a flash (I was to learn later that besides the high number of assault engineers killed and wounded there were also fifty-four RE other ranks missing).

Until that time I had never seen a live or dead German soldier in my life. Here suddenly were two of them almost jumping over me as I crouched low behind the sand bank at the high water mark. One of the Germans appeared to throw a hand grenade as he came over the top to land on the beach, although it was difficult to tell one explosion from the many others happening at the same time. Another British soldier must have thought a grenade was thrown because he managed to kick the German behind to send him sprawling, and then blasted away with his Sten gun. I figured that whether a grenade was thrown or not was hardly a matter for a board of inquiry in the circumstances!

I moved to a position to be able to view the ground over and beyond the sandbank. The area all around seemed to be covered by a burst of creeping barrages of shell fire, raging and rolling over the ground as if threatening to overwhelm all.

In the circumstances I decided to do something about helping some of the badly wounded soldiers – many of my own comrades among them – who were lying around in exposed positions on the beach. The best I could do was to drag a few of them to a low position in the sand dunes, where things were almost just as bad. I caught up with someone who had a stretcher, and the two of us worked as we never worked before. Truly in every way – emotionally, mentally, physically – the most awful job in the world. It was I suppose made worse for me because there were no medics around, obviously no hospital and no sanctuary other than a dip in the ground where we dumped those we carried. It is also true to say that quite a few of those who were placed there were hit a second time, some of whom were killed. I saw many mutilated bodies and grey – green – yellow faces on that morning; some who became silent and still forever. I was a stretcher bearer until I was physically exhausted, depressed and sick, when I could do no more. I handed over the stretcher to someone else, being firmly resolved in my mind that a stretcher bearer's job would never, ever again be one for me! Before moving away from the beach, my final effort was directed towards trying – though unsuccessfully – to plug a fist-sized hole in the back of another poor fellow who had himself been hit when tending to another wounded person!

Despite fierce fighting on the beach, within just over an hour, three exits had been cleared to allow the invaders through.

Thomas Kilvert and the 77 Assault Squadron were moving on to the village of Hermanville-sur-mer. At La Brèche d'Hermanville, German machine guns fired from trenches reinforced with concrete. Sergeant Kilvert reported:

We advanced in bounds to the high wall of the large farm. Here we split up into three parties, one covering the main road or killing zone, another as rear protection and the third as house clearance.

It was then that fire came at us from three sides, but bursts from our two Brens brought a lull. Shooting open the garden door, I advanced, covered by my Lance

> Sergeant and Sappers Lewis and Hand, up the two paths and raked the whole front of the house part of the farm with fire, killing, we found later, eleven of the enemy.
>
> We rushed into the house with hand grenades, and searched it from top to bottom. Going out into the yard we found the air raid shelter, and the civil occupants of the farm.
>
> Sapper Hand, who spoke the lingo, obtained the information that the big house (on the corner of Hermanville itself) housed about 200 of the enemy. I then reorganised the party, sending two runners back to Captain McLennen. Using the road ditch and the garden wall as vantage points, we advanced about 60 yards when Sapper Vaughan opened fire with a Sten gun on an enemy party coming down the road towards us.
>
> Immediately every one of us opened fire, and with the two Sgts with 100 round magazines on their Bren guns, this scattered the enemy.

By 9.30 a.m., the village of Hermanville was taken and the Riva Bella casino, a strongpoint, was captured by the Free French. However, the invaders began to face heavy German opposition and the advance was halted. With this resistance and the incoming tide, the beach became congested, holding up the reserve brigades. Around 1.30 p.m., commandos from the First Special Service Brigade linked up with the 6th Airborne Division at Pegasus Bridge.

The only German counter-attack on D-Day came from the 21st Panzer Division in the afternoon. This temporarily halted the British advance. At 9 p.m. more than 250 Allied gliders flew in to help defend against the German forces The 185th Brigade came to a halt at Biéville, 3 miles short of Caen, Montgomery's intended objective.

By midnight on the 6/7 June, 29,000 troops had landed on Sword Beach; casualties numbered 639, and a beachhead had been formed 6 miles inland.

Juno Beach

Juno Beach was 5 miles long and bordered by the villages of Saint-Aubin, Bernières-sur-mer, Courseulles-sur-mer and Graye-sur-mer. The first Allied troops to land on Juno Beach were the 3rd Canadian Division, led by 7th and 8th Brigades, and the 6th Armoured Regiment.

This invasion force was to advance inland and join up with Gold and Sword beaches on either side. The first wave of Canadian infantry, hampered by the strong current and bad weather, landed at 8.10 a.m.

Frank Lawson came to England with the Canadian Army in November 1941:

> My regiment was 13th Canadian Field Regiment Artillery: we had been told that we were landing on Juno beach, on an uncleared minefield, and that 50 per cent casualties were expected.
>
> There were ships, large and small, as far as the eye could see and we soon got our orders to fire, so at 1100 yards from the shore the guns of the Regiment opened fire onto the beach and all hell broke loose. As soon as the shell was fired, the case was thrown overboard. Shells were falling all around, no time now to be scared, the infantry had already landed, but the big guns in the German pillbox were trying hard to prevent the artillery from landing. At 200 yards from the shore, we were ordered to empty all guns and the landing craft turned back out

to sea. HMS *Rodney* was called on to silence the pillbox. On the second run, I saw a navy rocket ship fire a bank of 120 rockets and hit a plane flying across and they cut right into it. I saw the pilot's parachute open; I have often wondered if he survived.

I was the tank driver and we tried to get off the beach as quickly as possible to allow others to get ashore. There was a lot of German bombing and strafing, but our casualties on Juno beach were not as high as expected.

I can't begin to express the feeling of seeing so many dead, all young men in the prime of life, you could distinguish the Germans by their helmets; all somebody's boys.

At 8.30 a.m, Royal Marine Commandos landed at Saint-Aubin-sur-mer and headed east to join up with the British 3rd Infantry Division on Sword Beach. Again, the high tides and rough seas prevented attempts to clear the beach. Preliminary bombing had failed to take out the German defences. Soon the beaches were congested and under heavy fire.

Heavy enemy gunfire continued, but by 10.40 a.m. five beach exits had been cleared. After further heavy fighting, the beach exit at Courseulles-sur-mer was secured.

The Canadian 3rd Division was ashore by early afternoon and it advanced rapidly to join with Gold Beach to the west. By 8 p.m., troops had reached Villons-les-Buissons, 7 miles inland.

However, the link to Sword Beach, to the east, had not been made. Nor had another objective, that of capturing the German-held airfield at Carpiquet, been achieved.

As D-Day ended, a total of 21,400 troops had landed on Juno Beach; 980 had been killed, wounded or taken prisoner.

6

On the Beaches: Gold, Omaha and Utah

Gold Beach

Gold Beach, stretching for 5 miles, was split into four sectors: the assault would take place on three of them, running west to east, as the terrain in the fourth sector was not suitable for landings.

The aims of the assault from Gold Beach were to establish a beachhead between the towns of Arromanches-les-Bains and Ver-sur-mer; to capture the town of Bayeux and the road between that town and Caen, and to link up with the US forces coming from Omaha Beach. This would give the Allies communications from east to west.

As elsewhere, a naval and aerial bombardment was launched at German positions before the landings.

Bad weather and confusion among the Allied forces meant that some craft which were supposed to land in other areas were swept into the path of the Gold Beach troops. A high wind whipped up the waves, causing heavy seas; this delayed beach clearance teams and made it impossible for the DD tanks to land in the water, so it was decided that, instead, these tanks should be carried by their LCTs straight on to the beach.

Once on the beach however, as Austin Baker recalled, the tanks made rapid progress:

My memories of the beach itself are very confused. I remember noticing a number of DD tanks still there, but I couldn't see whose they were. Dabby, our commander, seemed to know where he was going fairly well, and in quite a short time we were off the beach altogether and going up a track with a procession of other vehicles. There were grassy banks on either side, and notices bearing skulls and crossbones and the words 'ACHTUNG MINEN'. In one place a big hole had been blown in the middle of the track and filled in with fascines.

Before long we were in Ver-sur-mer itself.

The village was quite a mess and about half the houses had been flattened by the naval bombardment, but the people still came out to cheer and throw flowers.

No firing seemed to be going on, and Benny, the driver, and I both had our heads stuck out of the hatches.

We went straight through the village and out at the other end and, quite suddenly, I realised that all the other vehicles had disappeared and we were alone. We were charging up a quiet country lane all by ourselves. I knew this was wrong because I had seen the orchard where we were to rendezvous on the map and I knew that it was on the very edge of the village. I told Dabby this and we had a bit of an argument – the first of many that I had with various commanders over similar things – before I managed to convince him. We turned round in a field, about a mile up the lane, and went back towards the village.

On the way back we met Muddy Waters with the leading troop of B Squadron, advancing up the road with their infantry. They had no idea anybody had gone ahead of them. The infantry had collected several Jerry prisoners from the fields and ditches.

When we got back to Ver we found Captain Collins standing in the middle of the road waving us into an orchard on the right. This was just opposite the original one, which had turned out to be mined.

Everybody seemed to have got there safely – Captain C. himself had got a lift on some other vehicle. One C Squadron crew was there. Their tank had been swamped on landing and they had lost all their kit and been soaked to the skin. They told us that it had been too rough for a DD landing and the tanks had done a deep wade instead, so all the months of DD training were wasted.

Sentries with Bren guns were posted round the orchard and then we had our first meal on foreign soil – tea, bully and biscuits, which we shared with the shipwrecked crew. Infantry were marching batches of prisoners down the road – a miserable looking lot, apparently of Mongolian type. A few shells landed in a wood across the road, but none came very near and nobody seemed to worry much about them.

I was surprised that there was no sign of the Luftwaffe. There were a lot of our fighter [aircraft] about in the new black and white striped recognition markings. Most of them were Lightnings.

Capt. Collins announced his intention of travelling on the ARV until he could get another vehicle of his own. I was rather pleased as he was a decent sort of chap and probably less likely to get us lost than Dabby.

Among those on the landing craft trying to reach the beach was Major Maurice Biddle:

We had our last communion in the well of the boat. After the service the padre asked me what he could do and I told him the roly-poly party was well under strength and asked if he considered that non-combatant duties. [The roly-poly was a carpet which was let down as the ramp was lowered.] I don't remember him answering the question; he just said, 'I go with them.'

We unshackled, the depleted roly-poly party took up the stations and we were now really running for the beach. Perhaps about 1,000 yards off shore I saw the LCT next but one to us, which was far up the lines as I could see, rear up and stop. I thought it was a hit. The next craft to us also reared up and stopped. Something resembling a telegraph pole with a large black box on the end slid past the side of our boat only yards away. We were really storming in. I was standing on the port fo'c'sle expecting a lot of small arms fire but it did not seem as bad as I had anticipated. 'Get up on to the fo'c'sles for the run in,' I called to the roly-poly crew, 'and keep your heads down.' They started to scramble up. About half of them had made it when we hit a mine. The German guns hadn't ranged us: the LCTs were hitting mines. When I read now of the wonderful briefings we had, I say, 'No one told me about these' …

… Up went the front of the boat; half my party were casualties. I picked myself up and we had to move the wounded. It was a bad start, particularly when we found that the explosion jammed the ramp. The front of the craft sank immediately although the stern was still afloat. We sledgehammered the ramp down, which took a few minutes and everyone jumped back into the vehicles …

> … Down the ramp went the roly-poly party into the sea and every man and the roly-poly were instantly swept away round the side of the boat.
>
> The small vehicles followed and all met the same fate. Hours later I did see the padre who said that he had got ashore several hundred yards down the beach but he knew nothing of the rest of the party.

The padre, whom Biddle refers to elsewhere as 'first-class', was Reverend Leslie Skinner, the senior chaplain of four attached to the 8th Armoured Brigade. Rev. Skinner recorded in his diary and memoirs efforts to help the wounded:

> Some casualties. Got Sgt Leades to bring half-track back to beach, hull down behind sand dune. Start gathering wounded, mostly infantry. More as day went on from further down beach. No news yet of any Beach Dressing Station. Regiment clear now and moving well. By midday concerned to pass on wounded … I saw skipper of large LST waiting for evening tide to float him off. Persuaded him to take more seriously wounded when he left on rising tide. By 14.30 hours got 43 on board – all carried by hand up 'Jacob's Ladder' and down near vertical companionways to crew's quarters. Terribly tiring. Sent radio message requesting our doctor to examine these wounded, if possible before leaving. He came about 15.30. Saw them all. OK except one likely to die before reaching England.

The high tide covered the beach defences of anti-tank devices and mines, which prevented the beach teams from clearing them out of the path of the forces coming in after them. At first, the invaders also met with strong resistance from the German forces but within an hour, three exits from the beaches had been cleared.

Major C.R. Whittington, known as Dick, was with the 1st Battalion Dorset Regiment, part of the 231st Infantry Brigade which attacked the westernmost area of Gold Beach. Shortly after landing, he wrote to his sister, who worked for the British Red Cross Society:

Dearest Joan,
The invasion was a wonderful experience. Of course we had had practices, exercises when we did the whole thing so that as far as getting on board ship etc., it was all very familiar. The amazing thing was the quantity of craft, the whole Solent was full of them, and many such unwarlike ones. There were dozens of destroyers, hundreds of LCTs, scores of LSTs lowering huge floats with cranes and bulldozers sitting on them. We were many days sitting there and when at last we moved it seemed hard to believe we were not just on another exercise. We had reveille at 4 o'clock and got into our LCAs at 5.15. The whole sea was full of ships, more and more were coming. The coast looked grey like any other coast. The weather was really beastly, cold and windy. We were nearly two hours in the boats forming up like some futuristic gala, the only signs of anger being a cruiser nearby steadily shelling away and further off some destroyers.

It was not easy to distinguish the coast. About half way in the music started – our music – high up we had aeroplanes. We could hardly see them but it was big stuff. Then crash and all the villages on the front suddenly grew immense plumes of thick black smoke. That seemed to open the beach and then our own field arty [artillery] started firing from their craft as they came in. 25pdrs make a good noise and the whistle of the shells [that] came over sounded very helpful.

My greatest concern was finding the right spot to land. Our boat was the leader and much devolved on us. Our MO, a very sound chap named Brown, thought he knew the spot but wasn't sure. Tony Jones, who was commanding that assault coy [company], was seasick and the whole place was covered in some. There were two landmarks sought – a little wooded farmstead about ½ mile back and a wreck to our left and 5 pill-boxes. Couldn't see any of them. In the end we got too far left.

Now just beyond the bank of sand dunes was a coast road with marsh on the other side of it. When we landed we had some way to walk from the boat … and bloody it was. Tit-deep with little rocks which were very upsetting – then the beach. All this while there were a few shells falling amongst the craft but no small arms fire up across the beach. We got down under the bank of dunes and then everything seemed to stop. We did not seem to know which way to go. I stuck up my flag and went to look. First left, then right, then I met the CO who said right was good, so left again, then right. This was when I got hit, and had to make my way forward to the farm, which was our assembly area, and got my assistant to take over the beach. The whole thing has been a sticky one for the battalion. Terry Jones who gave you dinner is killed, and Willie Hayes who came to meet you in his pyjamas is badly wounded by an air blast and probably blinded. I have been very lucky. How are you? I've heard and read

> great things about your doings. You've got the family flag held high. Well done, old bird ... I'm just about mended.

Within two hours, les Roquettes had been captured and, shortly after, La Riviere also fell. Resistance was fiercer at Le Hamel, but it too was captured by mid-afternoon.

Among the follow-up troops were the 6th Green Howards, among them Stan Hollis, a company sergeant major who won the Victoria Cross – the only one awarded on D-Day. Later, on a return visit, he described what had happened:

> The minefield extended from the beaches to the bottom hedge ... The platoon of D company were led through by the assault pioneers of the battalion. They went ahead with their 'hoover' things and laid the white tape behind them and we trod on the tape ... When we got through a hedge we started getting small arms casualties ... When we got to where [the] crossroads [were], we were getting more casualties. So then we got down and we crawled. We crawled up this hill and when we got here Major Lofthouse and I came forward to see what we could see. Major Lofthouse said to me, he said, 'there is a pillbox there, Sergeant Major'. Well, when he said that, I saw it. It was very well camouflaged and I saw these guns moving around in the slits. So I got my Sten gun and I rushed at it from here, just spraying it hosepipe fashion. They fired back at me and they missed. I don't know whether they were more panic stricken than me, but they must have been, and I got on top of it and I threw a grenade through the slit and it must have sickened them. I went round the back and went inside and there were two dead, quite a lot of prisoners. They were quite willing to forget all about

The niew from a landing craft as US troops attack Omaha beach on D-day. (Robert F. Sargent, US Coast Guard)

the war. The communicating trench from that pillbox to another one further along, and I could never understand, until a couple of years ago, how I got so many prisoners. I got eighteen or twenty prisoners. But we found out later that this was the command post for the Mont Fleury gun battery, which is just over the brow of the hill and this explains where all these chaps came from. Well, we didn't bother with escorts for prisoners, we just pointed the way back down the beach and they were quite happy to go by themselves and if you walk up to the pillbox you will see that it's still there.

Well, we came over this field here to advance to this Mont Fleury gun position, and it was at the top of that field that I looked back and I had been firmly convinced that the Green Howards were the only people fighting this bloody war. But when I looked back I couldn't see any water at all and it was then I realised that somebody else was helping us and all, and it gave us a great feeling of confidence. Anyway we advanced and as we appeared the Germans ran out of the back of the pillboxes. … It's now about half past nine in the morning. We got behind this mound. These chaps were starting to shoot at us from behind a wall and I saw a man running along the top of the wall, and I borrowed a rifle off one of the chaps and I took a shot at him and to my amazement I hit him. I had never been known as a good shot. If I fell down I couldn't hit the floor, sort of thing, but I knocked that man off the wall and at the same time I got hit in the face. Not a lot of damage. A lot of blood. It looked a lot worse than it was, and we went over there. The firing had ceased then. We found a man – a German soldier – had been just that minute killed so I assume it was the one I had knocked off the wall.

The whole company then advanced round the edge of that wall into the next village.

By mid-morning, seven beach exits had been established and British commandos had linked up with American forces.

As the day wore on, Austin Baker recalled:

> Everything seemed to have gone with a swing, but at teatime we found that this was not altogether the case.
>
> Two chaps from B Squadron arrived at our harbour – a corporal driver and his co-driver from one Lieut. Charlton's crew. They had gone over a rise and spotted a Jerry SP down the road ahead of them. They had fired and missed, and the next moment the Jerry had got them through the turret twice, killing the operator and wounding the commander and gunner. They had baled out and the two from the turret had disappeared somewhere (they got back, we found out later, but Charlton lost a leg). The corporal and his mate had walked all the way back to us – a distance of several miles. They were very much shaken up.
>
> Later in the evening Captain Monckton turned up. He too had been knocked out and wounded, though not severely.
>
> I discovered afterwards that A Squadron had had an even worse time that same evening. They had reached a place called Frenay-le-crotteur, quite a long way inland, and they had had four tanks knocked out by two 88s. TSM [Temporary Sergeant Major] Tabbs Davie's troop had had six men killed, including Tabbs himself, and ten wounded. Later one officer was killed and another wounded by a shell. C obviously had the easiest time. They had no further casualties that day after leaving the beach.

As D-Day came to an end, 25,000 troops had landed on Gold Beach. Casualties numbered 489. In the evening, Arromanches was captured and an advanced position stretching 6 miles was established. Troops from Gold beach had linked up with Canadian forces on Juno.

Arromanches was one location for the artificial 'Mulberry' harbours which Allied forces used to pour soldiers and equipment into mainland Europe.

Omaha Beach

The worst casualties by far on D-Day were among the 34,000-strong American forces which landed on the 5-mile stretch of Omaha Beach. This section of the Normandy coastline was bordered by 100ft-high cliffs, and Omaha Beach was the stretch of coastline which included the only breaks in those cliffs.

The objective for the invading troops was to establish a beachhead 5 miles inland, linking Port-en-Bessin and the British forces on Gold to the east with Isigny and American forces on Utah to the west.

The planned assault began badly, when 27 DD tanks (Duplex Drive – tanks adapted to start in the water), which were to lead the advance up the beach, sank in the heavy seas. Shortly after, the initial Allied naval barrage and aerial attack was launched on the German defences, but was of too short duration to be effective.

To make matters worse, only one of the infantry companies managed to land in the correct place. Others were scattered across the beach and many of the landing troops found that they were on sandbars and had to cross deep water to reach the shore. Laden with heavy equipment, many were cut down in the water by heavy fire. Smoke from grass set alight during the initial barrage obscured the landmarks which troops were told to look out for on landing, adding to the confusion as they came ashore. A key difference for the assault forces landing on American beaches was that they landed with fewer pieces of artillery and armoured vehicles.

By 7.00 a.m., engineers were struggling to clear obstacles. Among them was Dale L. Shrop, who was in a demolition squad of the US 1st Engineer Combat Battalion, attached to the US 1st Division:

> I was with the first wave at zero hour and one of the lone survivors of that day. I could not swim. When we jumped off the LCI, I was tied to my platoon sergeant with a nylon rope. Imagine being sent on this type of mission when I couldn't swim. I also had a life preserver on. It was not so humorous then because I was too scared to even know my name. A lot of the guys were hit below the waist and lost the use of their arms or legs, and the tide came in and got them before the medics got them. Another tragic thing I saw when I went back to the beachhead after it was secured – they had bodies stacked in rows like one would stack cordwood.

Melvin Farrell, of the 2nd platoon, Company B, 121st Engineer Combat Battallion recalled:

> The mission was to demolish a masonry wall about four feet high and four feet thick that ran parallel to the water's edge so that the tank forces could get in. Every man of us in the 2nd Platoon carried 40-lb. satchel charges of TNT for this purpose plus one 7ft Bangalore torpedo and full field pack, rifle and so on
>
> ... About 200 yards out our LCM floundered, nosed up on a hidden sandbar and stuck fast. The operator seesawed back and forth but she wouldn't give. The machine gun

fire rattling off the sides set up such a din of noise you could hardly think. The operator threw the ramp down and yelled, 'Hit it!'.

I was the 3rd man out. We three wheeled left and jumped off the side of the ramp. Machine gun fire was now raking the inside of the LCM, and a high percentage of our men were killed before they could get out.

...We landed in a shellhole and what with all the luggage we had plummeted to the bottom like a rock. We walked along the bottom until we climbed out of the hole...We were then on the barren sand but there was another stretch of water between us and the beach. This stretch contained a maze of tank traps, mines and every object the Krauts could plant to thwart a landing attempt.

I suddenly found myself confronted with what seemed a mountain of rusty barbed wire. I slid the bangalore as far under as I could, cut as short a fuse as I dared, lit it and ran back about ten paces and flattened myself out on the ground. It blew a gap about twenty feet wide in the wire.

This section was under intense fire from the pillboxes that we could see on the hill. Every fifth bullet used in machine guns is a tracer, which you can see in the form of a glow. These looked so dense and crisscrossed that it is hard to believe anything could get by unscathed.

With heartbreaking slowness I arrived at the wall behind which several of our men were already waiting for us. I threw my satchel charges onto the wall and attached the lead fuse to the primacord they had already stretched and started crawling down the beach for safety from the coming explosion.

When the explosion occurred, the first wave of infantry was about a hundred yards out. At this time our initial mission was completed so we huddled behind the ragged

Troops coming ashore from LCIs on Gold Beach, near La Rivière. (Sgt Midgley, No.5 Army Film & Photographic Unit. Crown Copyright)

remnants of the wall we had just blown. I turned my gaze toward the coming infantry and saw my Sergeant, Steve Kleman, not forty yards from me. He was sitting down, had been hit through both hips. I tried four times to get out to him to drag him in. Each time I left cover a hail of machine gun fire would drive me back. By this time he had been hit so many times it was hopeless.

Company B sustained 73 per cent casualties on this landing, but lying behind the cover of the wall we could not tear our eyes off the infantry. They ran through and up the hill in a never-ending stream, the dead and dying piling up behind them.

Six enormous coastal artillery guns on the cliffs at Pointe du Hoc were thought to be a major threat to the invaders. The guns would inflict severe damage on the advancing craft as they came across the Channel and could be turned on US troops who were to land on Omaha and Utah beaches. Divisions of the German Army were located nearby and could, with these formidable weapons, stop the invasion before it had got under way. Despite heavy air bombardment in preparation for the landings, the guns remained largely intact, so US Rangers were to climb the cliffs and deal with them. Covering fire was to have come from the tanks, nearly all of which had been lost at sea. Sergeant Leonard Lomell, leader of 2nd Platoon, 'D' Company, 2nd Ranger Battalion, US Army wrote later:

> After a stormy two-hour trip in our LCA, through cold rain and high seas and running the gauntlet for three miles, 300-plus yards offshore and under fire from the German soldiers on cliff-tops along the way, we Rangers finally fired our grappling hooks up over the 100-foot cliffs of Pointe du Hoc. Had we been on time, we would have caught the Germans asleep in their underground quarters, but we were 40-minutes late due to a British navigational error. [The Germans] were waiting to cut our ropes, drop grenades and shoot us down. We could not fire back or defend ourselves very well while climbing. Though we were seriously outnumbered, we prevailed.
>
> Shot through my right side as I led the men ashore in a wet landing, I suddenly disappeared in water over my head as I stepped off the ramp into an underwater bomb crater, which I could not see. I came out of the water with the help of my men, cold and wet, my right side hurting and arms still full of combat gear. We hurriedly headed

for the nearest ropes and up we went as fast as we could climb. There had been twenty-two of us in our British LCA, and we were all up the cliff within fifteen minutes, rushing through the German small arms fire as quickly as we could to the three gun emplacements that were our original objective on the west flank of the cliffs of Pointe du Hoc on Omaha Beach. The fortress at Pointe du Hoc had underground tunnels and troop quarters, and the Germans would pop up, firing their weapons from where we least expected. We moved on very quickly to avoid more sniper and machine-gun fire, as well as flat trajectory anti-aircraft machine-gun fire, which was becoming much more of a serious problem. We neutralised one German machine-gun position on our way across the point and temporarily quieted down the anti-aircraft position in order to get by it quickly and not get pinned down or delayed as we continued our assault. We got to our first objective in a matter or minutes after the assault; only the three guns in positions number four, five, and six were not there. Remember, there were no big guns anywhere on the Pointe's 40-acre fortress that we could see; only telephone poles or something similar sticking out of bombed out encasements. By this time we were taking mortar and heavy-88 fire, crawling fire to our rear. We moved out of that position fast, hoping to locate the missing guns, thinking they were in an alternate position inland and would soon be firing. It did not happen that way.

By the end of the day, the US Rangers had found and destroyed the guns, which had been moved inland. The links with Allied forces on Gold and Utah beaches had not been made. Over 34,000 troops had landed and casualties numbered more than 2,000.

However, Vierville, Saint-Laurent and Colleville had been captured and a small beachhead had been established which penetrated 1½ miles inland. US forces controlled all five access roads from the main Omaha Beach area.

Utah Beach

Utah was the name given to the most westerly area of the invasion area. It was just 3 miles long and stretched between the villages of Pouppeville and La Madeleine.

Five hours before the beach landings began, 13,000 paratroopers and glider forces were landed 5 miles inland and began fighting back to the beaches, clearing the way for those coming in from the sea. Unlike on Omaha Beach, the attack from the air was successful, but as the attempt to land on Utah Beach began, the guiding craft for the landing force was sunk and, without it, ships following went off course. The first troops came ashore at 6.30 a.m., south of their intended landing area, followed shortly after by the DD tanks. Fortunately, although the troops landed in the wrong place, they were in an area where defences were far lighter than the intended site; the Germans had flooded the coastal plain beyond the beaches and had fewer fortifications on this part of the coast. Almost all the US DD tanks came ashore successfully and dealt quickly with the light opposition. Most of the obstacles and defences on the beach area were cleared by high tide.

Captain Walter Marchand was battalion surgeon with the 4th Infantry Division at Utah Beach. His diary for 6 June begins early, with the sight and sound of the airborne assault:

D-Day is here! – D-Day has begun, how will it end? We are now close to the German held coast of France – all is unbelievably quiet, but it isn't for long. At about 1 A.M. I hear a low sounding drone – I go on deck and here I see plane upon plane flying over our ship toward the hostile shore, towing gliders – these are the Paratroopers and Airborne Infantry – I wish them God's speed and wish them well, for as I am watching the first planes are over the Atlantic Wall. I see tremendous flares go up and great quantity of anti-aircraft fire and flak. God what great numbers of planes there are, and all ours. To our right – toward the Barfleur Peninsula area our Bombers are wreaking havoc on some coastal installations, we can hear the detonations clearly. In the midst of this, the little Cavalry group is preparing to debark and to take St. Marcouf island – this is at H minus 4 hours. At this time also, the C47s are returning from France – flying home after letting go of their gliders or human cargo.

Had very early breakfast – then lay on my bunk for a while – I couldn't sleep and I can't sleep – I keep thinking of my wife and my family – I love you my Corinne.

At 0400 the first wave of our Assault Battalion is called to stand-by to load into the boats – there is a great hum of activity throughout the ship. The Captain speaks – our LCMs haven't come yet, but there is still plenty of time. We wait for 20, 40, 55 minutes. Then they come out of the dawn alongside – still enough time to make the H hour landing, for H hour has been upped because of the heavy seas. The LCMs are having great difficulty tying up to the boat – they toss around like corks – but the landing nets are overside and the troops make their way down – but with great difficulty. Often large hawsers,

2 inch thick, would snap like a thread and often the man climbing down would be thrown into the small boats. It was especially difficult to get the vehicles overboard into the small boats. 'Man overboard' was heard once – a British sailor was knocked overboard but rescued.

First wave – away, then the second, then the third, then it was my turn to get into my boat with five of my men and part of the Battalion Command section – it took long, the boat crashed against the ship time and time again, bending the ramp, and tearing loose, snapping the hawsers. Finally we are all in our boat with our equipment, and the men are getting seasick, and they huddle together toward the rear of the boat. I stay near the front of the boat, getting sprayed continuously and I look about me and see hundreds upon hundreds of boats, from the little [landing craft] to the huge battleships and cruisers, and smoke is billowing from their deck guns, for this is H-40 min. The Naval barrage starts then, the fire directed against enemy shore installations. Our wave has now formed and we are heading toward shore 7 miles away through rough waters, while on the way in, our dive bombers get to work, pouring tons of bombs against the enemy fortresses.

We are getting close to shore and the boats of our wave go from a line in file to a line abreast formation, and speed for shore. I can now hear cannon fire clearly as well as machine gun fire. We all pray that our boat will not strike a mine or an underwater obstacle or get hit by a shell from a coastal battery. All sounds become closer, when about 50 yards out, I see 2 splashes on our port bow – enemy fire. The boats streak for shore and hit the beach and we almost make a dry landing – we only have to wade knee deep through about 20 yds. of water. As we hit, the ramp goes down and we debark – wade in the water, then on hitting dry land [we] start to run. I see dead Americans floating in the water – a ghastly sight. I get my men together and we run up across the beach to a concrete wall, faced with barbed wire and bearing signs.

There are many wounded lying about and we start to care for them, and carry some to the Naval Beach Party Aid Station which just landed after us. I try to orient myself, but we landed at a different place than was originally planned. Enemy fire is increasing, landing just to our left, from our right there is machine gun fire. I have only one choice, I lead the men thru a break in the barbed wire into the minefield and we go in about 50 yards – enemy fire increases, we dig in hurriedly to rest – we are all exhausted from the fear which we all know as shells come whistling overhead and landing close by. But we must get out of the minefield! – I find a path to the right and we start along it, seeing mines all around us – and then the path disappears and we turn back to our former spot – from there we find a small path to the left and we follow it – we see wounded about us and we care for them, carrying some along with us on litters, and the small path leads us to a road and we follow it to the first right turn and we follow it.

Troops and vehicles are now storming ashore in great quantities – some vehicles are hit and burst into flames. We pass burning houses and many dead German and American soldiers. It is now noon – God the five hours passed like lightning. At 13.00 we come to the 'Old French Fort', now we are close to where originally we were supposed to land. I scout ahead and find my Battalion just 300 yards up the road, so I and Capt. Scott set up our aid station off the side of the road in a large hole and crater made by a 14 inch Naval shell – 12 feet by 5 feet and about 6 feet deep. By this time one of our Jeep ambulances has reached us and we are ready to function as an Aid station. We send out litter bearer groups into the minefields to pick up casualties. This is ticklish work, but the boys are excellent soldiers and go bravely although they have no paths to follow.

Our ambulance Jeep works up forward and brings back casualties – some are Paratroopers that are pretty well beaten up, having been wounded shortly after landing. We work from this spot for 2 hours and then we move forward to the Command Post which is along the side of a road near Fortress 74 which is still holding out. Shortly after arriving here, machine gun fire becomes active and we have to duck low – pinned down here for 5 hours, we could watch the attack on the fortress and the surrender of the Germans. Our boys are doing a splendid job and very few casualties so far. As the sun is setting we note hundreds of C47's again – more Airborne Infantry landing – they swoop inland and let go of their gliders, to come swooping back. Liasion Sgt. from Co. C shot in the leg while lying on the road beside Capt. Scott.

Toward dark a few serious casualties encountered – difficulty of evacuating great – plasma given right in open.

Difficulty in finding path through minefield to farm house where we will stay for the night – had to cross tank traps filled with water and lined with mines – ticklish business in the dark.

Finally we got all of the aid station together – we were all exhausted – and were so tired that we just fell down and fell asleep – with artillery, mainly enemy, going

> overhead, most of it, fortunately for us being directed toward the beach.
>
> This is the end of D-Day – it was hectic from the start – but we had few casualties, and those mainly from mines, which were numerous. Heavy machine gun fire heard all night.
>
> Pouppeville was captured by the afternoon and troops coming off the beaches linked up with the airborne forces.

The objective on Utah was to establish a beachhead from which the incoming forces could go on to capture the Cotentin Peninsula and, eventually, Cherbourg, the port to the north-west. By 10 a.m., six battalions had landed, and La Madeleine and the beach exits had been captured.

By the end of 6 June, over 23,000 troops had landed on Utah Beach and Allied forces had pushed 4 miles inland. Ground forces suffered fewer than 200 casualties.

7

Moving Inland

Allied soldiers and equipment poured across the Channel, to take the invasion inland quickly. It was vital for the Allies to establish their forces in Normandy, before the German counter-attack.

On the evening of 6 June, the British Prime Minister Winston Churchill gave the House of Commons a very positive report of the landings in France:

> ... during the night and the early hours of this morning the first of the series of landings in force upon the European Continent has taken place. In this case the liberating assault fell upon the coast of France. An immense armada of upwards of 4,000 ships, together with several thousand smaller craft, crossed the Channel. Massed airborne landings have been successfully effected behind the enemy lines and landings on the beaches are proceeding at various points at the present time. The fire of the shore batteries has been largely quelled. The obstacles that were constructed in the sea have not proved so difficult as was apprehended. The Anglo-American Allies are sustained by about 11,000 first line aircraft, which can be drawn upon as may be needed for the purposes of the battle. I cannot, of course, commit myself to any particular details. Reports are coming in in rapid

succession. So far the Commanders who are engaged report that everything is proceeding according to plan. And what a plan! This vast operation is undoubtedly the most complicated and difficult that has ever occurred. It involves tides, wind, waves, visibility, both from the air and the sea standpoint, and the combined employment of land, air and sea forces in the highest degree of intimacy and in contact with conditions which could not and cannot be fully foreseen.

There are already hopes that actual tactical surprise has been attained, and we hope to furnish the enemy with a succession of surprises during the course of the fighting. The battle that has now begun will grow constantly in scale and in intensity for many weeks to come and I shall not attempt to speculate upon its course.

In his memoir, T. Osbourne remembered arriving the day after D-Day on the Royal Navy rescue tug *Assiduous*, off Omaha Beach:

We were slowly making our way past evidence of sunken ships. American ships were alongside us. The crew told of the disaster ashore; they appeared very bitter. It seemed the soldiers were slaughtered on the beach due to the inadequate and poor aim of the bombardment.

A temporary grave had been dug at the base of the cliffs for the thousands of casualties. The ordinary American soldier and sailor were changed, as we all were, but the humour and high spirits bubbled through in spite of the ordeal.

The enemy was not far away and a large bombarding force was sending salvos over our heads every minute or

> so. The sound was of a screeching sigh. The smoke and flames were horrible to watch; the sound was the sound of death. We had orders to pick up a damaged landing ship at Utah beachhead a little to the west; however before we can leave a wire that was caught in our propeller must be removed! After strenuous efforts, this was accomplished.
>
> Utah was still under fire from enemy artillery when we arrived. Hits were being made on ships near us. Our tow was full of wounded. We secured the tow as fast as possible and made for the safety of the open sea.

In London, Alanbrooke was nervous. He wrote in his diary:

> The invasion is a day older. I am not very happy about it. The American Corps seems to be stuck. We are not gaining enough ground and German forces are assembling fast. I do wish to heaven that we were landing on a wider front.

Crucially, the response was delayed. German military communications in the area were so disrupted, that it was impossible for them to get an accurate picture of events. Furthermore, when news of the landings first reached his headquarters, at 3 a.m. on 6 June, no one would wake Hitler to tell him. General von Rundstedt, commander of the German army in Western Europe, could not order the Panzer divisions nearest to the invasion forces to move without Hitler's permission, which was not given until the afternoon.

The Allies' deception tactics were enormously effective and the RAF played a key role, as Wing Commander John Corby of RAF Tempsford recalled after the war:

> The D-Day Tempsford contribution was diversionary and made best use of our special skills. We were to assist in misleading the enemy about the location and extent of the landings in Normandy. We were to drop spoof troops and equipment on the eastern side of the Seine and into the Calais region. The histories relate here that Hitler and von Rundstedt continued for some time to think the D-Day landings were a feint and that the real thrust would come further north east so perhaps the Tempsford operation helped. The idea was that a quarter-sized parachute at one mile could be supposed at nights to be a full-sized one at one mile. We were therefore supplied with large numbers of manikins and small parachutes which were dropped in Rouen and Calais in designated areas. Accompanying them were a kind of assorted fireworks intended to go off like machine gun and rifle fire. Read like this the whole device sounds positively childish, and so it appeared to our crews. Nevertheless, they carried out the drops of course, and I believe they were quite effective on the ground and did in fact help to mislead the Germans. Later, at Staff College, I heard of the highly skilled operation of which we were really a part. Solely by elaborate flying and radar techniques the illusion was given to the Germans that a whole fleet of ships was crossing the Channel towards Dieppe and Calais. Our dummy men were part of this hoax.

Many of the German military commanders remained convinced that the 6 June landings were a diversion, and the real attack, through the Pas-de-Calais, was imminent. Messages from Garbo and a fellow double agent, codenamed Brutus (Roman Garby-Czerniawski, a Polish Air Force captain) appeared to confirm the rumours. Garbo told his German contacts some details of the Normandy invasion – too late for them to be of use -- and followed it up with this report of a meeting with his fictitious network of spies in Britain:

> I am of the opinion, in view of the strong troop concentrations in south-eastern and eastern England, which are not taking part in the present operations, that these operations are a diversionary manoeuvre designed to draw off enemy reserves in order then to make a decisive attack in another place. In view of the continued air attacks on the concentration area mentioned, which is a strategically favourable position for this, it may very probably take place in the Pas-de-Calais area, particularly since in such an attack the proximity of air bases will facilitate the operation by providing continued strong air support.

At Hitler's headquarters in Berchtesgaden, Colonel Friedrich-Adolf Krummacher, head of the intelligence branch of the Wehrmacht High Command added his own comment to the summary of this message: underlining the phrase 'diversionary in nature', he wrote, 'confirms the view already held by us that a further attack is to be expected in another place …'.

In the crucial early hours of the invasion, the only opposition to the Allies came from German forces already in the area. There was some fierce fighting but the German response was badly co-ordinated and the Luftwaffe had only a few planes in the region. The Allies established beachheads and the invasion began to move inland. Major John Rex was busy with landings on Sword Beach. In his memoir he wrote:

> Temporary headquarters of the Beach Group were in an orchard … There was little sleep. Enemy planes came into attack, which brought hundreds of ack-ack guns into action … Shrapnel fell in bucket loads, but the ugly night gave way to a perfect dawn … I met a lot of my old friends and I gradually took in all that the orchard held.
>
> Under hedgerows and fruit trees, holes were everywhere. Pioneers had dug down six or eight feet, huge oblong holes which were being used as offices, a telephone exchange, living accommodation and a cookhouse, and small ones were the officers' quarters.
>
> A mass of coloured signal wires were strung around and about the apple trees … There were enemy air raids every day and their batteries at Cabourg were causing us anxious moments. They got a perfect range sometimes on the beach activities and 'split us' in all directions. The Navy in anger concentrated ships' fire on these positions, but those heavy guns were never silenced.
>
> The Germans could see all our goings-on, stores and ammunition being discharged from coasters and freighters and landing craft pouring out more troops, more tanks and guns.
>
> Bombs set our dumps on fire and the petrol supplies were nearly destroyed, but the scheme of things as developed in England, went on around the village of Hermanville.
>
> There was a daily conference in the barn near the orchard, where, in the company of a horse or two and hens and chickens, the difficulties of organisation were

smoothed out. With the incoming tide, landing craft were called forward to beach. Ramps down, infantry men plunged into the sea, fully equipped. A supposed four feet, sometimes, unfortunately turned out to be more like six or seven. Men disappeared; they didn't come up. We did our best – there were rescues, but others – their bodies were washed ashore.

Freighters signalled their arrivals a few miles out and rhino ferries would put off to take their cargo of vehicles.

Tank landing craft pushed their bows into the sands and reinforcement squadrons were soon roaring their way in land.

... Amongst all the activity, heavy German shelling would break out and maybe our nerves 'danced' a little. At the back of the beaches, identification signs were constructed in large coloured canvas squares, superimposed on which were the military codes for our particular sands.

One part of the beach was a graveyard of wrecked craft, and tanks and armour from D-Day and just behind the beachhead was the drowned vehicle park, where a Recovery section was dealing with the mechanical casualties of the tide.

Here expert mechanics fussed over motors, trying to get a spark of life into them again. They had the tools and spares but it was a tedious job chopping and changing parts from one vehicle to another. The salt water had 'eaten' delicate parts, ruined the leads and wiring. Lifting the bonnet off one of these casualties which had been saved from the tide, gave one a filthy sight of sand clogged in every part.

Exits from the beach were constructed for wheeled and track vehicles, marching troops had their own way off.

Bulldozers did these jobs in very quick time. They also cleaned up the sands with their huge shining blades, pushing all litter, even cement blocks, into the back of the beach.

We took our meals where we happened to be. Midday we had a packet of biscuits, a canteen of soup, some rice or a slice of tinned pudding, washed down with tea, sat around the beach top. The sea air maybe improved the taste of everything; there was no doubt that the beehive of khaki enjoyed every morsel.

Ack-ack gunners had their holes and slit trenches in amongst us, with guns ready for action.

...These country roads were only wide enough to deal with a one-way traffic and so tender was their surface, so heavy the military movement, that sappers and pioneers were continuously patching them, with rubble from derelict houses and buildings ... The crossroads were enlarged and by-passes 'bulldozed' through the surrounding land, across wheat fields.

Convoys from the beaches and reception areas were continuous, like a ribbon unwinding, and for direction they followed a multitude of military signs and white arrows. The countryside was bursting with mechanical snails, resting, crawling, shading themselves under leafy cover. It was in reality a terrible war machine, which could snarl, growl and roar, shew its flaming jaws in bitter and sustained action.

The maintenance area, where all war stores were dumped, was having its difficult moments to keep movement 'fluid', and we had our headaches working out the answer to the problem of avoiding congestion ... To casually glance at all the lorries creeping and resting like insects amongst the various stacks, was to imagine

> that ample time was on hand, but ordnance officers were just wearing themselves out ... We all got back to headquarters in the orchard at night pretty weary, as there was no 'let-up', the war game was being played morning, noon and night, every day.

On 7 June, Douglas Heathfield-Robinson, a driver with 297 General Transport Company, Royal Army Service Corps, arrived 5 miles off Juno Beach. By now the routine was established:

> When the order came to leave the ship, the first DUKW [amphibious lorry] had to reverse out ... once off the ramps it sank beneath the waves. Luckily the two drivers managed to escape and were picked up out of the water. After this episode we were full of anticipation, it was my turn next with my co-driver Andy Date.
>
> I drove gingerly onto the ramp and slowly edged the DUKW into the water. With the engine revving I engaged the gear for the prop shaft and with the propeller spinning we sank into the sea and started floating. We had never been trained for this kind of thing. Once we were away from the LST, we edged our way to the two church steeples in the distance and made our way to the shore. On reaching dry land we reported to the Beach Group Officer, who gave us directions as to where we should unload our cargo – this was done by a large lorry crane.
>
> To think that the invasion had only started 36 hours previously. It was difficult to realise an invasion had taken place at all, apart from gunfire in the distance, and a few wrecked ships that had been sunk by enemy action and a few battered tanks.

Universal carriers, with screens for deep water, passing through the coastal village of Lion-sur-Mer on 6 June 1944. In the background is a Churchill AVRE. (Sgt J. Mapham, No.5 Army Film & Photographic Unit. Crown Copyright)

At sea there were many craft, including cargo ships, battleships and then we saw it, the Queen Mary hospital ship moving among the fleet of ships.

The sun was shining down, everywhere appeared quiet except the damaged houses that now came into sight. The thing I shall always remember is the stench of dead cows lying around with their feet in the air like upturned tables, killed either through shells or bullets. Eventually the poor creatures were buried by bulldozers in large graves.

We were given orders to report to the Chateau. This was the company HQ. Here we found the reason for our delay [getting] ashore was the fact that the 3rd Canadian Division we were attached to had had to repulse a fierce counter attack by the 21st Panzer Division who had joined the battle, so we were unable to come ashore until the area had been cleared. [On the afternoon of D-Day, the 21st Panzers had attacked British forces at the village of Ranville and by the evening, had driven a wedge between the British and Canadians, reaching the coast at the town of Lion-sur-Mer.]

Once unloaded, the next thing we had to do was dig slit trenches. Having never been to a war zone before it was difficult to realise that we would have to sleep in these trenches; they had to be at least 2ft deep. We were in a small orchard not far from the beach, [and] after eating part of our 24hr ration we got down to sleep. After being at sea for five days it felt great to be on hard ground again.

About 2am the following morning we were woken up by a massive air raid, in spite of being told that the Germans had no aircraft. The ground shook with massive explosions and apart from ordinary bombs, we were deluged with butterfly bombs, which exploded on impact or to touch.

> Sadly that night we had 7 lads killed, 30 wounded by shrapnel and some 30 of our vehicles damaged by shrapnel. Now we knew we were in the war zone.
>
> The dead were buried next day by the Pioneer Corp chaps 303 company and the wounded were shipped to the hospital ships by DUKWs.
>
> The DUKWs were repaired during the day by our hard-pressed workshop group [and] by mid-afternoon they were all operational again.

His role in the deception over, General Patton told the US Third Army which was following up on the initial landings:

> I don't want any messages saying 'I am holding my position.' We are not holding a goddamned thing. Let the Germans do that … Our basic plan of operation is to advance and keep on advancing regardless of whether we have to go over, under or through the enemy.

But the landscape made progress difficult . From the coastline to about 50 miles inland, the countryside was typically made up of small fields, bordered by thick hedges and earth banks, with narrow sunken lanes between them.

The defending German infantry, armed with rockets and anti-tank weapons, could hide until the enemy was at very close range.

Austin Baker was moving inland on 7 June and finding evidence of German troops everywhere he went:

> We bowled off up the road and seemed to go for quite a few miles without seeing any signs of activity. However,

the front was obviously in rather a fluid state, and the fact was soon brought home to us forcibly. We passed a line of ambulances which were standing at the side of the road – their crews made no attempt to stop us. We had gone about a hundred yards past them when suddenly Freegard, in the back, opened up with a Bren. I had been in a bit of a dream for a few minutes and I came to with a start. Benny turned the ARV round and we hared off back down the road. Freegard said a gang of Jerries had appeared in the field on our right. I believe there had been a Jeep ahead of us and somebody had seen a couple of blokes bale out of it into the ditch. I don't know what happened to them, because we carried on past the ambulances without stopping. On the way back to harbour we passed a self-propelled gun which Collins had encountered the night before. It was a 75 mounted on a Mark IV chassis. I didn't fancy looking inside, but Freegard had no qualms and even fished out a very battered and blood stained Luger pistol.

Near Ver we gave a lift to an infantryman and half a dozen prisoners on their way back to the PoW cage at the beach …

On the way through Ver, Benny hit a wrecked house, and brought a whole wall crashing down across the front of the ARV. I had my head sticking out but, by a remarkable bit of luck, I was wearing a tin hat for about the only time in the entire campaign. I found myself lying on the floor under a pile of rubble, a bit dazed but otherwise none the worse … Knocker Bell was there and he told me that 5th troop, which was my troop, had had a very bad time that afternoon. As the squadron was harboured not far away I decided to go along to them and find out some details.

I nearly got lost on the way, as I had to pass through a thick copse and, in one place, through a sort of tunnel of undergrowth. It was getting dusk, but I eventually found them, and saw McGuirk almost at once, badly shaken.

The worst piece of news was that Wally Walters had been killed. Wally had been my closest friend ever since I joined the regiment and his death was a terrible blow. Four of the others had been killed as well and one badly wounded ... On this first day, a formation of about a dozen fighters came over ... Everybody said that they were FW 190s, but they looked like Typhoons to me, though I couldn't see their recognition markings. Anyway, several machine guns in the neighbourhood opened up and Captain Collins had a go with a Bren. Unfortunately he tripped over while he was firing it, and the gun slewed round and sprayed the orchard with bullets. It was a wonder half of us weren't killed, but nobody was hit and neither were any of the planes.

Rev. Leslie Skinner was working with the medical teams inland from Gold Beach:

Wednesday, 7 June 1944 (D-Day plus 1)
Up at 4.30 hours. No time or opportunity for wash. Beach been heavily bombed during night. Attack by squadrons and infantry on Bayeux going well. Nothing doing at Regimental Medical Aid Post so borrowed a motorcycle (my own being unusable through 'drowning' when half-track landed from LST). Went back to beach checking on casualties and seeking news of those 'missing' – who are mostly members of crews of 'swimming ranks' of C Squadron.

Arrived on beach at 08.00 hours, met Padre Scott (whom I knew well) of the Beach Group and helped him choose a burial ground while we were under rifle fire from somewhere not too far off.

Saw one or two of our wounded. No news of Lt Hills or his crew or others of C. Squadron. Saw Lt Bridges of the Brigade Forward Delivery Squadron who had got 10 tanks ashore out of 13 with loss of two men drowned.

Met Gladstone, Corps Padre, just arriving about 11.15 hours. Back to Regiment and found HQ moved. Caught up with them in outskirts of Bayeux 15.00 hours. Met Brigadier seeking RHQ and led him in.

Town almost cleared now. From 20.00 hours, occasional rifle fire, not close. Squadrons leaguered outside Bayeux, which is now taken. We (Medical Aid Post) joined them. Some shelling nearby. Good wash and bed about 00.30 hours.

Thursday 8 June 1944 (D-Day plus 2)

Up at 04.15 hours. After wash and breakfast moved several miles SE. In action for first time as a Regiment, with Infantry support instead of in separate Squadrons.
Attack on point I03 between Audrieu and Le Pont Roc overlooking River Seulle above Tilly. Started fairly quiet mostly recce in wretched tank country. Occasional shelling and mortar fire from enemy. Many isolated enemy infantry positions and snipers.

06.00 hours attack on hill proper. Open ground across railway line deadly to cross. Tanks moved fast. Medical units wait in wood behind.

09.25 hours two high explosive shells in quick succession in entrance-gap in wood. Seemingly our cover not so good. Cpl Sadler, MO's Radio Op., wounded

Riflemen of the 1st Battalion Royal Ulster Rifles, 6th Airborne Division, drive past an Airspeed Horsa glider on 6 June 1944. (Sgt Christie, No.5 Army Film & Photographic Unit. Crown Copyright)

> above left ear and chest. Sgt Loades and self, tin hats punctured – Loades some concussion, self scratches only. MO's half-track radiator shattered. Evacuated Sadler and Loades to ADS then towed MO's half-track to rear of wood where regimental aid post continued to function.
>
> Late evening Lt Verner brought in, sniper wound behind left chest – serious. Doctor dressed wound and I helped evacuate Verner to ADS riding on rear door and bumper all way holding bottle giving blood drip – nearly five miles of rough going to 75 Field Ambulance unit at Marigny. Cramp arms/legs awful. Journey back in dark, nightmare. Doctor had moved again. Found him by 01.30 by which time feeling tired somewhat faint. Bed on ground by 02.00. Shelling during night. Heavy bombing on beaches. Disturbed sleep. Up at 04.30.

Before leaving for Normandy, Rev. Skinner had met Keith Douglas, the best-known poet of the Second World War. He later told Douglas's biographer, Desmond Graham, that he 'had set up his field altar beside Douglas's tank as the most convenient place in the Squadron's line ... and after the service [Douglas] stayed to communion'.

That evening, to Skinner's surprise, he joined the civilian congregation in the small village church – the only soldier there. After the service, he came up to speak to the padre and they walked in the New Forest, talking of Douglas' conviction that he would not return from Europe.

Rev. Skinner recalled:

> He was not morbid about it. He could talk of and make plans for the days when the war would be over, and having done so come back again to this feeling that it was

unlikely that he would survive ... We walked and biked together only separating as the dawn was breaking.

The story continues in Leslie Skinner's diary:

Friday 9 June 1944 (plus 3)
News of death of Captain K[eith] Douglas on forward slopes Pt. 102. CO refused permission for me to go forward to recover body – enemy dug in with tank support. Two drivers of A Echelon taking up replenishments wounded. Helped bring them in – then evacuated loads. Back 20.00. News death Lt Peter Pepler on same slopes as Douglas. Clearing area forward of Pt. 102 effective but costly. Tanks forward ¼ mile on downward slopes to allow infantry and anti-tank to dig in and cover approaches to St. Pierre and Tilly sur Seulles – ditto on left towards Fontenay and Cruelly.

By midnight our tanks pulling back, refuel etc, leaving one Squadron in open leaguer to hold the hill.

Remaining tanks joined A.Echelon at Brecy above and south of Cruelly near St. Gabriel. All safely in by 02.00 hours. Stayed up to see tanks in and check casualties etc. Bed by 03.00 after few sharp words with CO about not being allowed forward to recover bodies of Douglas and Pepler.

Later, in his memoir, Rev. Skinner wrote:

Keith had done a reconnaissance on foot with a fellow officer. As they returned across the fields the two separated to go to their respective tanks. As Keith drew near to his tank there was an outburst of enemy shelling and mortar fire and Keith was killed. When I finally recovered the

> body I was surprised to discover it was quite unmarked. I could only conclude that he had been killed by the 'airburst' of a high explosive shell quite close above his head. I buried him close beside the hedge near where he was killed. There was no possibility of doing otherwise. Being quite alone and reading the brief Order of Service over the grave affected me deeply.

That same day, T. Osbourne was crossing the Channel back to England to collect a 'Phoenix', part of the artificial harbour under construction off the Normandy beaches. He recalled later:

> Following re-provisioning and refuelling, we proceeded to Selsey Bill for orders. Three men were missing; they were entered in the log as deserters. No one commented on this for none of us knew if and when we would reach our own breaking point ... Our tow was to be one of the concrete monoliths. As we made our way through the dozens of concrete blocks lying silently waiting to be taken in tow, it was as though we were in a city of lost men. I had an eerie feeling, and although my shipmates laughed when I voiced my feelings, their laughter sounded hollow.
>
> We left Selsey Bill with a concrete block at nine o'clock in the morning. We now knew they were called Phoenix units, presumably because they could be sunk on to the seabed and raised again by compressed air pumps.
>
> We were in convoy to the shore of France after picking up our tow from the city of concrete blocks. Over 100 tugs were involved [and] the blocks [were] soon to be known to the world as 'Mulberry Harbour'. We proceeded in line

with the Dutch tug *Swartz Zee*; sister ships of ours, *Sesame* and *Allegiance*, and two American tugs, the *Partridge* and *Algoma* which completed our little armada.

Our Canadian escort gunboats sped about like mother hens; although, in truth, they were very small compared to the monoliths they were towing …

On the 11th June, enemy aircraft appeared over the convoy in the early hours of the morning. We gave them a heavy reception, and all but one left the area. This aircraft dropped chandelier flares over the tow. The plane came in again and crossed our path; we felt very vulnerable, fully expecting bombs to come hurtling down. However, the plane flew off. The flares still hung in the sky, lighting the sea for miles around. Explosion after explosion occurred: HMS *Sesame* was engulfed, as was the USS *Partridge*. We passed through the floating debris.

During the night we were issued with Benzedrine tablets to help keep us awake.

[On] 12 June 1944, we were at Arromanches, which was in the British Gold beachhead. Arromanches is where William the Conqueror had built some of his boats for the invasion of England in 1066. Now it was the site of Mulberry B. Our tow was moved into position under a terrific bombardment.

Off the coast of Juno Beach, on 8 June, the blockship *Empire Bunting* was being prepared for detonation, as subaltern A.J. Holladay noted in his diary:

As soon as fighter cover disappears – at midnight – fun begins. Enemy aircraft over beaches and terrific Bofors barrage goes up. Red chains of floating lights covering the sky for mile like a Brocks Benefit display. We open on a FW and an Me [German planes] which come our way and score a hit on the FW. Other guns then open on it too, and it finally crashes. Day shows 2 or 3 LCTs sunk, one with broken ends sticking out of the water a quarter mile away. One destroyer badly hit – funnel gone. We are untouched. Cruiser of 1943 class leads in big troopships and commences to bombard shore targets again. We move in closer to shore and RN officer begins to plant the Gooseberry. An assault landing craft mysteriously blows up a few hundred yards from us and disappears with all hands. Late in the afternoon hearing explosions on the beaches – shelling seems to have begun at last. Once again no Luftwaffe. Shelling turned out to be detonation of landmines on beaches by Royal Engineers. Thank God for that! At 21.30 we weigh anchor and move into position for Gooseberry 4. At 23.00 the merchant crew is taken off in Yankee tug; we stay on and they blow us all up. Ship settles smoothly, but main deck almost entirely awash. Life is going to be very uncomfortable. Sleep in crowded wireless cabin. Men huddle on bridge, very nervous and irritable, waiting to be taken off. Another terrific barrage and we put up a noisesome smokescreen.

One week after D-Day, Captain Maurice Jupp, who had landed in a glider with the 6th Airborne Division, wrote to his parents:

Somewhere in France, 13 June 1944
… I am so sorry that I could not write before. Until tonight I could only find time for only one or two

postcards. I will not speak about the operations we have been involved in: we are allowed to say so little, whereas the accredited war correspondents can write any bilge they like. Judging by one or two papers I have seen, (several days old, of course) they have allowed these boys a lot of licence: I had a good laugh at the D Mirror that described solders getting their mail on D-Day: one unit has had some mail for the first time today; the rest of us hope to get some tomorrow.

The inhabitants have had a pretty bad time during the last 7 days. Many of their homes have been destroyed and their cattle killed (by shrapnel etc). Nevertheless they are strongly pro-ally, and do all they can to welcome us. I am very well but in need of a bath and more sleep. I hope that you are both reasonably well. Soon I hope for time to write more interestingly.

Out at sea, A.J. Holladay's work on Gooseberry 4 continued, but on 19 June, the weather deteriorated:

Woke to really dirty day and the heaviest sea I've seen. The ship is moving very considerably on the bottom – shifting and swaying – which is very unpleasant. Our decks are completely engulfed and the waves are terrific. At least this should get rid of the filthy oil that has been on our decks for two weeks. All the small craft rush to our shelter but lengthen their hawsers and lie discreetly off when they see how we are shifting. Our stern is brushing against bows of 308 and plates on both ships are buckled. We drift quite a way apart from next ship towards Bob, and the bridge shattered. Cook compo lunch in wheelhouse.

At low tide we lay hawsers to neighbouring ships to try and hold us steady in the night. Wind still blowing gale force in the evening. What a bloody life! As tide rises again in evening storm grows in ferocity and lashes water over boat deck, tearing up the decking and flying bridge. Steel hawser holding us to next ship parts. Water comes lashing up round bridge. Nasty moments. We huddle up on top bridge and wait for events. Number of landing craft in great distress. Danger of our breaking loose and smashing all craft in our lee. Only 3 ropes holding us forward now and terrific strain coming on them in snatches with the waves. Turn in at midnight.

20 June (D+14) midnight
No air activity in the night. Storm continues, if anything, worse than before. Only one rope holding now. Morning tide brings water up to the level of boat deck and just below my cabin. Flying bridge completely smashed, broken in two in a second of time. Half the planking of the boat-deck gone. Water halfway up the superstructure. Warmer but wind stronger. Rocking and swaying of ship all morning. Cooks in fo'c'sle so no food. Our penalty for becoming bored! Detail on gun cut off on duty for six hours. Eventually we all get lunch at 3pm. New moon tonight. Tide comes very high indeed and enters my cabin. Also enters fo'c'sle and wireless cabin. Men in fo'c'sle get on forepeak where they are drowned in waves and spray and huddle miserably together, clinging to rails to avoid being swept away. Wireless operators climb on top of wireless cabin and are half-drowned and buffeted there. We get on top of bridge. Power of sea simply terrific – slowly smashing the boat to pieces. Send SOS

to 324 and barge picks up men from fo'c'sle. Wireless ops can't be rescued and they spend a bloody night soaked to the skin and in considerable danger of being swept away.

21 June (D+15), Wednesday
Air raids during the night but we are cut off from our guns! Most of the party on the bridge turn in, in the wheelhouse but I prowl around waiting for the tide to go down. Do a lightning kit pack in middle of night and cart valise and boxes up to bridge. Tide goes down eventually at about 3.30am. Find wireless ops soaked through and all sleeping on one bed at back of cabin. Rest of cabin completely wrecked, including wireless sets. Ask Bob to have us taken off in morning. American tug comes alongside at 8.30 and takes off selves and some kit. No time for stores. Our only meal for 17 hours has been a few biscuits and a lot of rum. We get across to 324 and I go on board. Kit is taken over to 205 and in process my box is dropped in water. Goodbye to 600 cigarettes and all my changes of clothing. Soaking wet and have only what I stand up in! Cart my valise across assault course from 205 to 324; it is completely soaked too. Life saved by cup of tea on ship and excellent lunch (fresh meat!) and bed made up by the resourceful Biddle. Men's accommodation on 324, 205 and intermediate ship – very poor, sleeping on floors of saloons etc. Ships are all packed with Marines whose landing craft have sunk or gone adrift. Gale continues unabated, several landing ship tanks go in, but all smaller stuff has been held up for 48hrs! Position becoming serious. When will ruddy gale die down? Send back party of 3 with Sgt Longden to 410 to guard kit and bring it over eventually. Excellent

tea again. Weather still rough as ever. Talk to RASC capt and HAA lieutenant from a Rhino which was adrift for 13 hours and has been waiting 2 days to unload. Tales of the gilded life in Cairo's European hotels and bars from RASC captain. Visit men on all ships and find them in much better humour – living rough but glad to be off 410. Bollock them about rifling of NAAFI pack. Turn in early – delicious to be on firm dry ship!

22 June (D+6), Thursday
Storm has subsided a bit but sea still choppy. Some blue sky. Go ashore with Gunner Williams and mail in LCVP. Land at Courseulles harbour, which is now full of craft and full of workmen putting it in order. Walk to 114 RHQ at Grange-sur-Mer and meet CO and Major Carline, whom I knew on *Spartan*. Have lunch with them, get some maps, and leave note of supplies required. No mail for us still! Walk back to Grange and after delay find LCVP returning to Gooseberry. Dusty roads in sunshine, roses in the garden where we had lunch, quite a few civilians about – including a girl or two. Back in very choppy sea (wreckage of craft all along the beach) and tricky job getting from ML back on to Gooseberry … Phillips has brought back Longden's party with stores from 410 and reports extensive additional damage. Plan to remove 40mm and gunstores. Weather breaks at last: calm sea and sunshine in evening, terrific unloading activity.

G.A. Wildman was a junior RNVR cypher officer off Sword Beach in HMS *Largs*. HMS *Largs* was a Combined Operations Headquarters ship, manned by Navy, Army and Royal Air Force communications personnel, in addition to the usual Naval crew: 'Our work in the cypher office was very heavy and it was a case of work, sleep and eat. Consequently three of us who were to go ashore were only too anxious to do so if only to get more rest,' he wrote to his wife. Once on land, he had discovered why a colleague had written to him from 'The Hole in the Ground':

> … the office consisted of a dugout covered by stays and a tarpaulin such as a cover from a heavy motor lorry. It was fresh and healthy so long as the weather was good but the day after my arrival the weather broke once more and the whole place was soon a sea of mud. In the same grounds was a chateau which had been used by the Germans as a sort of H.Q. Our staff occupied this and it was intended eventually that we should move in and use the place as an office while continuing to live under canvas. On several of the walls were quite large drawings by the previous German occupants, one of which depicted Stalin and Churchill evidently in some deep communistic plot. On the other side of the field in which we worked was an orchard – in good weather it would have been an ideal spot to spend a month or two.
>
> As I came ashore later than the others, I was accommodated in the RN Camp some five or ten minutes walk from my place of business. Since then many of the officers have left and today I have a very comfortable tent complete with table, wash stand and some rather pansy curtains bequeathed to me by the previous tenant. All the tents in which we sleep are dug in to a depth of four or five feet as protection against splinters and blast. Much of the shelling has subsided now but until a few days ago we lay in our beds at night while a two-way traffic of enemy

shells and shells from our warships at sea passed over us. It is not a very bracing experience but not I imagine so bad as the doodle-bugs [flying bombs] which I am sorry to hear you are having at home. One of these latter by the way passed over our camp the other morning, heading south at a height of about 2000 feet. It must have been one of the better types which could not identify its target and was therefore returning to base.

Whilst ashore I have had the opportunity of seeing some of the German defences and hearing accounts of how the Jerries behaved. First as to their conduct before the invasion. I am told that generally speaking it was very correct – in this district they brought much of their own livestock and paid the local people a fair price for goods they bought. Many of the German soldiers had French girl friends. Although there had been elaborate preparations against invasion the war had from many points of view not touched the local people to any marked degree. In peacetime this was a holiday resort and for miles along the coast there were pleasant little houses which today are nothing but heaps of rubble. From what I heard we did effect a large measure of tactical surprise which seems rather amazing but I think the weather was such that a landing was not thought possible. The French people round here who very wisely took to the countryside during the heavy bombing which preceded the landings say that many of the Germans in the coastal defences abandoned their strong points and retired inland where they caused great confusion by impeding the German reinforcements which were moving towards the beaches. Some of them of course stayed on. There was one strong point consisting of a huge armour protected

> dug out, the iron door of which was jammed. Several attempts to open it were made without success and it was eventually left until D plus 4. When the steel door was eventually forced about 30 Germans walked out to surrender – they were fully equipped with a wireless and plotting instruments and had been radioing information to the Germans for some days. Even as late as a month after D-Day one German was caught in one of the houses on the beach – he also had been sending information to the Germans by wireless. He was spruce and well fed and once spotted surrendered without any trouble. The beaches were heavily mined and in addition there were various obstacles such as stakes driven into the beach. Off the beaches, the verges were heavily mined with kindly notices from the Germans bearing a skull and cross bones to remind all and sundry of the fact. Now the German guns are abandoned and everywhere there are signs of the heavy pounding which the place has received from the RAF and from the artillery. Here and there are burial grounds with white wooden crosses to mark the last resting place of our dead.

On 7 June, Canadian forces captured the villages of Authie and Carpiquet from the 12th SS Panzer Division. Counter attacks continued for five days before the Panzers were finally driven back.

Six days after the beginning of the invasion, the Allies had established an offensive line along the Normandy beaches.

The two Mulberry harbours, at Arromanches and Omaha Beach, were in operation by 9 June. The Omaha harbour was destroyed in the storms of 19 June but the harbour at Arromanches was repaired and continued to land thousands of tons of supplies daily. By 4 July, one million men had been landed.

There was fierce fighting in the difficult terrain. Allied naval and shore-based artillery were met with counter-attacks from German artillery and from the air. Allied airforces gained control of the skies and attacked German reinforcements.

By the end of June, American forces had taken control of the Cotentin Peninsula and the city of Cherbourg, its harbour and fortifications.

The German High Command kept two armoured divisions and 19 infantry divisions in the Pas-de-Calais throughout July and August 1944, still waiting for a second and larger Allied invasion.

8

Casualties and Non-combatants

At the time of the invasion, Colette Day was a teenage girl living in the old city of Caen. In her memoirs, she recalled how, on 7 June, the war came to her home while the family was eating lunch:

> Everything looks normal, yet the air is electric. There are tomatoes and hard-boiled eggs as a starter, followed by cold chicken left from Sunday. But before we start the second course, an alarm interrupts our meal and is followed so closely by the planes and the sound of the first bombs that we leave everything on the table and rush to the shelter. It is 1.45pm. An attack has never been so close and violent before, it takes us by surprise.

After a second raid, they come up to view the damage:

> Our bedroom is unrecognisable. The window is just a gaping hole with torn net curtains. My toys have been thrown all over the floor. The wardrobe is badly damaged, the mirror shattered, it does not look like the same piece of furniture and I stand there for a while looking at it ... But there is no time to lose, I must think about what I should take. For the last few months we have had a suitcase ready packed, just in case ... As time passed and

> nothing happened, we took more things out of it until only clothes I have grown out of remain.

Colette's mother prepares to leave and begs her parents to come with them, but they refuse to leave the hotel. When the guests have all said their goodbyes, Colette writes:

> Now we are four left. My mother, almost in tears, is accusing grandfather of wanting us all to die. She does not want us to part. It is awful, I want to go too, but I don't want to leave them. So I join mummy in trying to persuade them to come with us. At last grandmother gives way. We know she is making a huge sacrifice, for she would rather stay with her husband and the possessions she worked hard all her life to acquire, but she understands we won't go unless she leaves with us for we have always depended on her judgement …

They set off for the home of friends at Fleury, a village 4 miles away on the outskirts of Caen:

> When we reach the top of our road and cross the Rue Saint-Jean we realise how lucky we have been until now. So many houses are destroyed. The house where my school friend lives in is no more, nor is the newsagents where we bought our daily papers. What happened to the people living there, are they dead? Are they buried alive?

They arrive at the house in the evening. The next day, her grandfather joins them:

> He seems back from the dead, he is lost and defeated. Still, we are together again, we are so happy ...

He tells them that many civilians are buried under their houses. The hotel is still standing but all the houses around are ruined and most are on fire.

> We will never see our home again. I must have been mad wanting to stay behind, it's hopeless, we are ruined.
>
> Tears roll down his black stricken cheeks making long white lines, I've not seen him cry before, grandmother holds his hand and for a short time there's silence. Nothing one can say would efface our misery.

During the first twenty-four hours of the invasion, more then 800 people died in Caen. Field Marshal Montgomery had hoped to capture the city on D-Day, but German forces concentrated on holding it over the following weeks. Intense Allied air raids and British naval bombardments began, and a controversial air raid on 7 July destroyed the old city, killing 350 civilians. By the time Caen fell to the Allies in July, a total of 1,150 civilians had died in the bombing and fighting.

In England, Allied casualties from the invasion began arriving at the Isle of Wight advanced casualty clearing station within hours of the start of the invasion. Ambulance driver M.E. Littleboy wrote:

> ... there was no time to think, and we didn't know which way to turn. Back and forward, to and from the quay at Yarmouth, fetching in casualties off boats returning from France. My first case I remember in particular, racing down to the quay and backing up by the water's edge

and waiting for we knew not what. But when they did arrive it was pitiful, one was unconscious, the other had a fractured skull and badly cut face. Both shot-up naval casualties. But never am I to forget the pathetic dazed expression on the face of the conscious one. He was very young, only a boy, but the look of bewilderment and suffering was too awful in one so young.

All night and day we did this for British, Americans, Merchant Navy, Army, Navy, Air Force, mostly shell wounds and loss of blood. The Red Cross boat was magnificent and worked day and night, with always the same crew and MO. Unshaven and unwashed, they were hunting for lost ships and never returned until they had found them. Sometimes we would go to the quay at 12pm and wait there until 3 and 4 in the morning until we saw the boat coming in.

The nights were eerie down there with only an orderly to keep one company. They would be clear and starlit, and perhaps a siren would go, and the rumble of guns would be constant and the roar of our own planes would swell the din.

The lights would move along the sea – another convoy going out and signals would flash out their vital messages. Then a little red star would appear and gradually draw nearer and slowly the Red Cross launch would bump alongside and the tired and weary men would lift their casualties into our ambulance.

Maureen Bolster served in the WRNS as a courier at HMS *Mercury I*, a shore establishment at Haslemere, and saw men returning from the Normandy beaches. She wrote to her fiancé (later her husband) Eric, an Australian pilot officer with the RAF:

WRNS Quarters June 9th 1944
Dearest Eric,
My goodness I wouldn't be on leave at this time! Thank God everything is going quite well.

It is wonderful to see the men coming back – dirty, unshaven, some suffering from shock in varied degrees, others cheerful and wanting to get back. They've all tremendous tales to tell.

One officer got back here from a port on another coast wearing his officer's cap, flannel bags, a dreadful old jacket and moth-eaten brown carpet slippers!

Another broadcast last night on the 9 o'clock news. Perhaps you heard him.

We've been on the films too! The first invasion newsreel!

Naturally the place is a hotbed of rumours but I only wish I could tell you what we know to be true.

On Wednesday night there was a dance here. Heaven knows I didn't feel like dancing with all that hell going on not so very far away but something inside told me to go and help bring a little gaiety to relieve the tenseness of the atmosphere. So another Wren and I went along. I'm glad I went. I hadn't been in there long when a lad of about 18 or 19 slipped into the hall and sat beside me. I took one look and knew where he had been. His eyes were bloodshot and red-rimmed, he was shaking like a leaf …

Poor kid, all he could say to me was, 'make me forget it, please make me forget it … I've just got to'. I felt quite sick with pity, Eric. I looked after him all evening.

He'd just had his 19th birthday. At first he was incoherent – but as I nattered trivialities, he gradually got better. He was upset because his mother would be worried. What the kid had seen was beyond telling. For one thing, he'd seen his special pals blown to pieces. By the end of the evening he could hardly stand for exhaustion, so I put him in the care of a PO who promised to put him to bed. Just as I was leaving 3 ruffians came in, filthy, bleary-eyed, unshaven – they just stood there. No-one seemed to take any notice of them. I didn't know them but I went up and said, 'hello, I'm terribly glad to see you back', and one just looked at me, and sort of sobbed, 'God you don't know how pleased we are to see you, Stokie!'

And do you know, Eric, a large number of the Wrens have NO interest whatsoever in the crews because they're just plain common men. They only associate with officers!

This morning I spent selling Red X flags to them all, and the tales I heard and the tea I drank!

Nothing one can do for those men is too much.

Lots of German prisoners have been turning up on these parts. Rozelle has seen hundreds of them. She said they looked awful, just like animals.

We thought we'd be bombed all along the coast but nothing's happened ...

... I should think leave will start in about a month for those who haven't had any for some time, so if you can come in the next month or two, I might get some compassionate leave with luck. Perhaps the old war in Europe will be over this year – oh roll on that day! I seem to want you home more and more every day ...

All my love,
Maureen

Captain Jupp wrote to his parents about the life and the civilians in Normandy:

17th June 1944

At last I have the time to write at reasonable length. Things are quiet today here; the sun has come out this afternoon; cows are dotted about the fields in front of us, chewing forcefully: apart from the soldiers, their dugouts (I have a fine one here) and the odd bang now and then, and Spits flying over in 4's, everything is incredibly peaceful.

Later I shall be able to tell you a bit about our operations: for the moment, I can say nothing about them. However, I can say one or two things that give nothing away. I had better not describe the journey or our landing. The reactions of the French were interesting. Most seemed remarkably unsurprised to see us. Some said, 'Bonjour' as if they saw us every day, although certainly others rushed up and shook us by the hand. An old woman came up to me and held out 2 new laid eggs: I took them. That would not happen now: early on, a farmer offered me eggs any time I liked to call for them. I met him 4 or 5 days later and he told me that the noise had put his hens off laying and any they did lay were immediately swiped by our men.

They all seem to accept damage to their houses and injuries to the population as inevitable. Of course, as a nation, they're used to their country being devastated periodically by war.

Since I started this letter I've had a very welcome bath (cold) in a rubber dinghy filled with water – 8 of us bathe in it.

... I have seen no fat French children: the ones I see, without exception, even in the country, are thin. I'm sure in the towns they doubtless are thinner. The French rations are very considerably less than the British. The food we get is excellent: unfortunately we eat too much. I feel guilty about this with the French not getting enough.

It is getting too dark for writing. I'm glad to hear you are both reasonably well.
love Maurice

Captain Cross also found the local population welcoming, even though they knew the Allied landings meant danger:

The French people I have met have been marvellous, very pleased to see us – pleasure mixed with apprehension because they knew that when we arrived it might mean shelling, it might mean we have to raid their houses to protect ourselves, it would assuredly mean the death of a lot of their livestock. This is a horse and cattle breeding district, and one of the saddest things is to see their carcasses lying about, nobody having time to deal with them – fields full of very scared animals, some of them wounded. The local drink is cider, rough but very good and I hate to think what goes into the making of it. However the alcohol in it makes it safer to drink than the water hereabouts. The civilians used to give us cider if we asked for a drink. Recently though we have not been near any places with inhabitants about ...

... A very touching scene yesterday. I went back to revisit a farm I once occupied for a couple of days and where we made ourselves very popular and were very polite. They fell on my neck and called me 'Their own Lieutenant' and were very pleased to see me, because we behaved so much better than the people who took over from us – loaded me with vegetables, cabbage, carrots, onions and lettuce and would only accept a few cigarettes and a bit of tobacco in payment.

Transport moving across the Caen Canal Bridge at Bénouville on 9 June 1944. A crashed glider is in the trees. The bridge was renamed Pegasus Bridge after the mythical winged horse, the emblem of the British airborne forces which took the bridge. (Sgt Christie, No.5 Army Film & Photographic Unit. Crown Copyright)

On the Isle of Wight, ambulance driver M.E. Littleboy ended her diary on Friday 16 June:

> … my last journey to the mainland with casualties – a never to be forgotten trip … They were burnt so badly as to be unrecognisable, only the burning eyes could one see, and as we loaded our stretchers I could feel those eyes following me round the ward. I tried to smile at them, my

smile was stiff and I felt sick, and though I was so full of sorrow for them, something inside me just seemed horror struck. One of our patients was a boy merchant seaman, who couldn't have been over 16. He was tiny and as light as a feather and I noticed on his label 'shell wounds'. My admiration rose. My load consisted of 3 stretchers and one sitter. The small boy, an American airman shot down, who looked so pale and fragile and shocked, and a British major ... He had a gangrenous leg, but was the best patient of the lot. My sitter in front was Major McClure, who had shell fragments in his ankle and foot. The two majors were what is known as bomb happy; this is almost a kind of disease. They were the craziest of spirits, though obviously nervy with it. They were both Desert Rats and had been through the Italian campaign ... and how I ever managed to keep my bouncing major in check I do not know. The hospital staff saw them off with deep regret and we started off for the ferry. The policeman threw them all roses, and so we made our way on to the boat, amid much laughter that I was not to drive over the side. So began my journey to Portsmouth. The sea was so rough that the water drenched the ambulance and we had to shut all the windows. But there was no keeping Major McClure inside and it was he who pointed out the various sights etc. Firstly masses of pontoon bridges, thousands of them all ready to be towed across the Channel ... There were boats everywhere with literally only the length of a boat between each, all the way to Portsmouth. Tank landing craft and troopers, air-sea rescue boats speeding along – cruisers and battleships. The *Nelson* looking magnificent and the major said only the day before she had fired behind them as they touched the beaches. Landing craft of

> every variety painted almost every variety of gay colours due to camouflage and looking like some regatta with the flags flying. The horizon was thick and black with boats. One couldn't imagine where they all came from. It was never-ending, we needed to wheedle our way between them. My patients used their field glasses and were highly excited. Indeed it was a wonderful sight.

For Wren Barbara Bruford, the invasion marked the end of her job at Portland Bill, listening in to the enemy's transmissions across the Channel:

> … once D-Day had come and gone, Portland had really no purpose. We [had] listened to [the enemy] for months reporting convoys – theirs and ours – but once the British landed, the lighthouse personnel retreated fast – some of them cursing their sergeants and some of them pouring out terrified messages for their families when they realised that they would be taken prisoner.
>
> When they had all gone it was the end for Portland. Gradually people were drafted away to other jobs, and I was left to close down the station.

Despite the surprise of the landings and the lack of a co-ordinated response by the German military, both sides suffered very heavy losses on D-Day. Modern estimates of Allied casualties on D-Day suggest a minimum of 10,000 killed, wounded or missing. Casualties on the German side for this first day are estimated at between four and ten thousand.

Operation Neptune, the codename for the Allied invasion and establishment of forces in Normandy, continued for the rest of June. Despite the Allies' vastly superior numbers,

A Conundrum, or cone-ended drum, for laying PLUTO (PipeLine Under The Ocean), which kept the Allied invasion forces supplied with fuel. (Author)

the Battle of Normandy (Operation Overlord, of which Neptune was part) took far longer to win than the Allies had expected: fighting carried on until the end of August, when German forces retreated over the River Seine and back to Germany. By this time, French Resistance fighters had led an uprising in Paris, and the city had been liberated by French and US forces.

During the Normandy campaign, more than 200,000 Allied troops had been killed, wounded, or were missing, as were at least that number of German troops. A further 200,000 German troops had been taken prisoner.

Across Normandy, as the Allies advanced, civilian casualties were also high. French civilians fled their homes in towns and cities to avoid the fighting. Even so, at least 15,000 were killed during the landings and estimates put the total number of civilian casualties for Operation Overlord at over 50,000, mainly as a result of Allied air raids.

Sources and Further Reading

Original Papers

Imperial War Museum
Ackroyd, M.W.
Baker, Austin
Beal, Kenneth
Bolster, Maureen
Bruford, Barbara
Carruthers, William
Cass, E.E.E.
Corby, John
Cross, C.T.
Cutler, W.
Day, Colette
Dickinson, Ivan
Fenwick, C.
Gadsby, Shirley
Geddes, Rosemary
Heathfield-Robinson, Douglas
Holladay, A.J.
Jupp, Maurice
Kilvert, Thomas
Lane, A.J.
Littleboy, M.E.

de L'Orme, Maximilian
Oakley, Kennet
Osbourne, T.
Owen, Veronica
Rex, John
Skinner (including Maurice Biddle), Leslie
Whittington, C.R.
Wildman, G.A.

Personal Communications

Gwyneth Verdon-Roe
David Clark

Websites

Air Mobility Command Museum http://amcmuseum.org
Black Hills Veterans Writing Group www.battlestory.org
Veterans Affairs Canada www.veterans.gc.ca
D-Day: Etats des Lieux www.6juin144.com
D-Day Overlord www.dday-overlord.com
D-Day Museum www.ddaymuseum.co.uk/
Pegasus Archive www.pegasusarchive.org/
WRNS Association /www.wrens.org.uk

Books

Barber, Neil, *The Pegasus and Orne Bridges: Their Capture, Defence and Relief on D-Day* (Pen and Sword, 2011)

Blandford, Edmund, *Two Sides of the Beach: The Invasion and Defence of Europe in 1944* (Airlife Publishing, 1999)

Carey, John (ed.), *The Faber Book of Reportage* (Faber, 1987)

Crowdy, Terry, *Deceiving Hitler: Double Cross and Deception in World War II* (Osprey, 2008)

Danchev, Alex and Daniel Todman (eds), *War Diaries 1939–45, Field Marshal Lord Alanbrooke* (Weidenfeld and Nicolson, 2001)

Duboscq, Geneviève, *My Longest Night: An Eleven-year-old French Girl's Memories of D-Day* (Leo Cooper, Pen and Sword, 1984)

Freeman, Ray, *We Remember D-Day* (Dartmouth History Research Group, 1994)

García, Juan Pujol and Nigel West, *Operation Garbo*, (Biteback Publishing, 2011)

Grogan, John Patrick, *Dieppe and Beyond: For a Dollar and a Half a Day* (Juniper Books, 1982)

Howarth, David, *Dawn of D-Day* (Companion Book Club, 1960)

James, M.E. Clifton, *I Was Monty's Double* (The Popular Book Club, 1957)

Miller, Russell, *Nothing Less Than Victory* (Penguin, 1994)

Morison, Samuel Eliot, *History of United States Naval Operations in World War II: The Invasion of France and Germany* (The University of Illinois Press, 2002)

O'Connell, Geoffrey, *Southwick: The D-Day Village that Went to War* (Ashford, Buchan and Enright, 1994)

Zaloga, Steven, *D-Day Fortifications in Normandy* (Osprey Publishing, 2005)

Index